Counter-deterrence

Gerald R. Wheeler

Counter-deterrence

A Report on
Juvenile Sentencing and
Effects of Prisonization

With a Foreword
by Leslie T. Wilkins

Nelson-Hall   Chicago

47861

Library of Congress Cataloging in Publication Data

Wheeler, Gerald R
   Counterdeterrence: a report on juvenile sentencing and effects of prisonization.

   Bibliography: p.
   Includes index.
1. Juvenile corrections—United States.
2. Indeterminate sentence—United States.
3. Juvenile justice, Administration of—United States.

I. Title.

HV9104.W478   365'.42   77-26975
ISBN 0-88229-315-X

Manufactured in the United States of America

10   9   8   7   6   5   4   3   2   1

CONTENTS

FOREWORD

It is a long time since we were honest enough to admit that we put people in prison to punish them and that prisons are useful places for getting "them" out of "here." We do not use this kind of statement now. Though we send offenders to the same kinds of places and do much the same kinds of things to them, it is recognized that this is no longer punishment; it is "treatment." Institutions of incarceration are no longer called prisons, but correctional establishments, and at times we go even further and call them "medical facilities" or "training centers." In other times, certain offenders were put in the stocks so the populace could see them and have a little fun with them—punishment by ridicule augmented with a little acceptable physical inconvenience in the form of rotten eggs and other light missiles. But the open punishment of offenders is no longer regarded as a fit entertainment for the public; "treatment" is better carried out where it is not visible.

The major change in penal practice in the last few decades has been in terminology. We have ceased to call a spade a spade. Instead, it has become a "manually operated implement for something-or-other." Criminal justice agencies have gone even further from the paths of linguistic honesty than mere embellishment by excessive redundancy. More subtle yet radical inexactitudes have been necessary to disguise both the lack of development of procedures and the failure to achieve any of the objectives of justice. Consider, for example, a few of the transformations: the "punishment block" is now the "adjustment center"; "solitary confinement" is recognized as "therapeutic isolation"; there is no such thing as "forced labor," rather, we have "work therapy," "character training," and "inculcation of habits of industry." Hardly an honest descriptive term remains in the language of the field of criminal justice, from its first move towards the suspect (for example, "preventive police patrol") to the parole agent's supervision and surveillance of his case-load of "clients." It is possible to give only a few examples of the language reform game; its use often passes unnoticed. (Did the reader note that pelting a prisoner in the stocks with rotten eggs was termed "acceptable physical inconveniences"?) Language reform is cheaper than change of procedure, but it is also dangerous.

Justice and honesty would seem to be concepts which should get along well together; when they do not, one may suspect that something is wrong. And, indeed, it is.

In our presentday society, we like to think that we give special consideration to the young. It is generally assumed that benevolence epitomizes our dealings with the young offenders and others of a tender age who are in need of care and protection. We assume that there would be no need to camouflage what is going on in such places as Youth Training Institutions. This is not so. It may even be that the situation is worse in the young persons' institutions than in prisons, since children are not regarded as adults and, hence, are not entitled to the full legal protection and rights that adults enjoy.

On occasion, the courts have removed the lid of security from some young persons' institution. The revelations should have shocked us into rethinking the procedures of so-called "rehabilitation." Some examples may be useful here.

Noting that the intercession of "a federal court into a state correctional system is a matter of such gravity that [it is] not done here lightly," Chief Judge Pettine, in the United States District Court, Rhode Island, in July 1972 (Civ. A. #4529—*Inmates of Boys' Training School et al.* v. *John Affleck, Director, Department of Social and Rehabilitative Services, et al.*), found that "isolation of juveniles in cold, dark isolation cells containing only toilet and mattress . . . constituted cruel and unusual punishment. . . ." The plaintiffs made, among other pleas, prayers for relief, which, Chief Judge Pettine observed, raised questions about the philosophy of treatment of juvenile offenders and about what rights juveniles retain in their confinement at state correctional centers. Opposing the plaintiffs' request for (among other things) a full day of schooling for those under sixteen were such persons as the Commissioner of Education and the Superintendent of the Boys' Training School! It would appear that, in this matter, they were on the wrong side! The defendants sought dismissal of the action "for failure to state a claim on which relief may be granted" (Rule 12(b)(6), Fed.R.Civ.P.). They also asked that the court "abstain from decision." The court, however, did not find that the case presented any issues of state law, the clarification of which would "obviate the need for a federal constitutional decision or would present the federal constitutional issue in significantly altered light."[1] Some excerpts from the record of this case will serve to provide a dramatic backdrop for the research reported in this book and for the suggestions for reform which the author puts forward.

> There are no specific rules or regulations which indicate what offenses will result in transfer of a juvenile to Maximum Security. . . .
>
> There is evidence, and I so find, of at least two probable suicide attempts by boys who received no medical or psychiatric care proximately following the attempts. The response of the BTS [Boys' Training School] supervisors to these suicide attempts was solitary confinement. . . .
>
> Two of these cells are stripped isolation cells, containing nothing but a toilet, and a mattress on the floor. The cells have, at times, not had artificial lighting. In one of the cells, the window is boarded over, rendering it completely dark at times. These cells are known as "bug-out" rooms and are used for solitary confinement of boys. . . .
>
> . . . he observed a boy attempting to hang himself. He managed to get the boy down. Requesting instructions and assistance from his superiors, the staff member was told to put the boy in the "bug-out" room. He did. Once in the room the boy started banging his head into the wall. . . .

---

1. These would be the grounds for the court to "abstain from decision."

Is this merely an isolated example of juvenile "training procedures" in the smallest state and, hence, atypical or unique? It is apparently not unique. Texas can provide another case in *Morales* v. *Turman* (Civil action #1948 E.D. Texas: August 1974: 364, F.Supp. 166: 1973). Two institutions, known pleasantly enough as Mountain View School for Boys and Gatesville School for Boys, were ordered closed by the court on account of information presented. While the court declared that the practices were brutal and violated due process, the Superintendent of the Gatesville School for Boys stated, "We do not have any punishment for discipline. We have punishment for control, if you want to call it punishment; we use force for control." (It is interesting to see the language game in action again in this and other statements.) Let me quote a few further items from the record as it appears in the Federal Supplement (#364).

> Widespread practice of beating, slapping, kicking and otherwise particularly abusing juvenile inmates in absence of any exigent circumstances in many of Texas Youth Council facilities was violative of state statute, avowed policies of Council, and the Eighth Amendment against cruel and unusual punishment. . . .

> Use of tear gas and other chemical crowd control devices in many Texas Youth Council facilities in situations not posing an immediate threat to human life or an imminent threat to property, but merely as a form of punishment, constituted cruel and unusual punishment in violation of the Eighth Amendment. . . .

> Placing of inmates confined to facilities of Texas Youth Council in solitary confinement or secured facilities, in absence of any legislative or administrative limitations on duration and intensity of confinement and subject only to unfettered discretion of correctional officers, constitutes cruel and unusual punishment in violation of the Eighth Amendment. . . .

> Requiring inmates confined to facilities of Texas Youth Council to maintain silence during periods of day merely for purposes of punishment and to perform repetitive, nonfunctional, degrading, and unnecessary "make-work" tasks for many hours constitutes cruel and unusual punishment. . . .

But, is this not again just an unusual case—a dramatic incident which serves only to prove, by exception, that most youth facilities are rehabilitative and safe places of detention? Clearly it is not known how widespread are the abuses of power in the name of "treatment," "training," "rehabilitation," or "therapy." However, *Nelson* v. *Heyne:* United States Court of Appeals: Seventh Circuit (491, Federal Reporter 2d Series—case decided Jan. 31st, 1974) is another recent case which raised some serious questions about practices in the state of Indiana. The Indiana Commissioner of Corrections was the defendant in this case. Again, it seems necessary only to extract some materials from the record and let them speak for themselves, without embellishment.

> Corporal punishment administered in medium correctional institutions for boys twelve to eighteen years of age, consisting of beatings on the buttocks with a "fraternity paddle" causing painful injuries, was disproportionate to the offenses and constituted cruel and unusual punishment. . . .
> We are not persuaded by the defendant's argument that the use of tranquilizing drugs is not "punishment." Experts testified that the tranquilizing drugs administered to the juveniles can cause: the collapse of the cardiovascular system, the closing of the patient's throat with consequent asphyxiation, a depressant effect on the production of bone marrow, jaundice from an affected liver, sore throat, and ocular changes. . . .

As Justice Fortas had noted earlier:

> There is evidence, in fact, that there may be grounds for concern that the child receives the worst of both worlds; that he gets neither the protections accorded to adults nor the solicitous care and regenerative treatment postulated for children. (383 U.S. at 556, 86 S.Ct. at 1054)

Cases of the kind quoted may be examples of a basically good system which has failed in some specific cases. The very fact that action is taken by the courts to remedy the malpractices may be asserted to demonstrate that the system is working, as a whole, extremely well. It should be noted, however, that the cases we have considered are of recent date and represent a large state, the smallest state and a medium-sized state, from the north, midwest, and southern parts of the country. It may also be questioned why, when a case has been presented, defended, and lost by an agency in one part of the country, similar agencies in other parts have not learned by the example and modified their procedures so that further cases would not have to be presented, argued, and proven, and local remedies ordered in relation to reliefs sought by their inmates. It may be that this happens because the correctional agencies, and especially those dealing with juveniles, really believe that what they are doing is in the best interests of their wards. Thus could one agency come to court and defend their use of a "fraternity paddle," while another defended their use of drugs, which the court found to be dangerous and the administration of which to constitute cruel and unusual punishment; thus, indeed, was it possible for still another agency through its personnel to defend the use of isolation "bug-out" cells. It is even probable that there was a strong belief, sincerely held, that such cells were an appropriate form of "treatment" for a malady which demonstrated itself by the "symptom" of attempted suicide.

The concept of "treatment" makes it unnecessary to consider questions of due process, or to balance the punishment to the seriousness of the crime, and renders it irrelevant to notice questions of fairness and equity. Is it possible to imagine a case where the term "treatment" is appropriately used—where the medical model applies—and the issues of due process arise? The very concept of "treatment" as coercive is the enemy of "justice."

The indeterminate sentence is, of course, a logical necessity of the "treatment" approach to the disposition of offenders. It cannot be known in advance how long it will take for the "treatment" to be "effective," and since there is no question of an appropriate balance of punishment and crime, there is no limit of time for the continuation of the "treatment." A pleasantly simple and persuasive argument can be made for keeping offenders out of society for as long as they present any "danger" (i.e. until they are cured), and at the same time there is no point in retaining a person in "treatment" (incarceration?) once he is "cured." There is, of course, considerable difficulty in defining the terms used in this argument. When, for example, is an offender "cured"? When is a "criminal" no longer a "criminal?" What exactly is "dangerousness"? How is it to be measured in terms of probability and severity and at what level is incarceration to be expected? How are the symptoms to be assessed and dealt with?

In this book, Dr. Wheeler presents an examination of the assumptions and impact of the indeterminate sentence (with its attendant "sickness" model of crime) upon the juvenile offender. He considers also the implications of the indeterminate sentence on controlling or reducing crime and delinquency in society. He sets forth some evidence and argument that the indeterminate sentence may work in the opposite direction to that which any simple hypothesis might postulate. He suggests that the present system is counterdeterrent and probably destructive. It is easier to take the mystery out of the idea of "punishment" than it is to ensure that democratic controls are applied to the working of any "treatment" model. It is the function of democracy to guard its citizens (which would, in our view, include children and young persons) from arbitrary coercion by the agents of government. Furthermore, citizens have a right to know what institutions of punishment and justice are doing, and to know this in such terms as permit of estimates of probable impact upon themselves and others.

It is possible, of course, that state agencies may carry out effective treatment, but the criteria of this must be more firmly established than mere belief that it is so. Even well-established and scientifically proven methods of treatment may be unjustified if they imply coercion.[2] Coercion is punishment. It is

---

2. There are serious problems in any system which attempts to combine "punishment" (even assuming that it is well justified and commensurate with the crime) and "voluntary treatment." The situation which involves punishment can hardly leave the subject with as many degrees of choice as he would have were he not at the same time in receipt of punishment. I think it is possible to justify a combined form in *logic*, but not in practice.

possible to justify punishment, but not on the same terms as treatment. As soon as a case hits the criminal justice system, it is assumed that other agencies of social control have failed. It would appear that there is a need for system-to-system feedback of some complexity rather than mere allocation of blame to individuals or dispensation of "treatment." The delinquent is, by his act, commenting not only upon himself, but also to a greater or lesser degree upon society and its institutions.

The child welfare system, as it works at present, has a marked tendency to concentrate its correctional resources on the young and more trivial offenders, and even upon the nonoffender. The evidence of this is in this book.

Dr. Wheeler does not stop at mere criticism of the present state of knowledge and practice. (This would have been a safe thing to do!) He puts forward suggestions for development of noncoercive "treatment" in the community. His arguments for this are worth careful study and consideration. A great need exists for innovative thinking about ways for dealing with offenders of all ages. We can be sure of only one thing. More of the same—more of what is now being done—will not do! Whatever is to be done in respect to offenders, whether they be young or old, should be such that it can be regarded as "fair." If it is first of all "fair," then it may also be "just."

In my view, the concepts of (a) crime and offenders, (b) individual responsibility, and (c) personal dignity and autonomy are closely related. The use of other frames of reference for our consideration of criminal behavior can so easily lead to degrading the human personality. The clinical medical model, which leads logically enough to coercive "treatment," while still popular with those who claim to be humanitarian, is, I think, no exception.

It should always be kept in mind, however, that criminal behavior cannot be excused, and that, furthermore, the problem of crime cannot be simplified to the problem of the criminal. Neither the punishment of offenders nor their "treatment" has had much impact upon the frequency of criminal acts. We must diversify our approach. We should seek ways to deal with crime and its threat and damage to society and the individual victim. No matter how severe the punishment of the offender, the victim is not benefited to any degree, and usually the situation remains unchanged, only to generate further crimes by other offenders. Merely tracking down offenders and finding them guilty, plus some form of disposition, will not suffice to ameliorate the crime problem.

Crime in society is a problem to be solved, not a thing to be attacked. It is not a simple matter, but is as complex as human behavior itself. Neither fear nor anger provides a suitable mental set to assess the issues involved. A strategy of problem solving in this area has yet to be developed. More studies of the kind presented in this book will provide the beginnings of a humanitarian, yet scientific, approach to some of the serious problems of how to deal with delinquent youth.

> Leslie T. Wilkins
> State University of New York
> Graduate School of Criminal Justice
> Albany

PROLOGUE:

Toward the Dismantlement
of the
Therapeutic State

Youth in trouble are governed by the therapeutic state. The rule of law and moral judgments has been replaced by what Kittrie describes as the therapeutic state—a hybrid system of social defense founded on classical and deterministic views of crime.[1] The former stresses egalitarianism, free will, and individual responsibility. It imposes penalties in proportion to the crimes. Determinism, the dominant view, maintains that penal sanctions are inappropriate because "either persons were born with criminal behavior patterns, or their social climate induced criminal tendencies."[2]

In order to protect itself, Kittrie says, society quarantines delinquents and other social misfits in the therapeutic state. Here, under the *parens patriae* power of the state, deviants are entrusted to the "curative" power of science and exempted from criminal sanctions.

> Within this system, little or no emphasis is placed upon an individual's guilt of a particular crime; but much weight is given to his physical, mental or social shortcomings. In dealing with the deviant, under the new system, society is said to be acting in a parental role (*parens patriae*)—seeking not to punish but to change or socialize the nonconformist through treatment and therapy.[3]

Exile to the therapeutic state has been facilitated by the divestment of criminal justice in the name of humanitarianism. Release is predicated on successful completion of treatment and cure. The fact that treatment is involuntary and the cure is a hoax is immaterial. The goal of the therapeutic state is not justice but conformity and experimentation. To achieve this end, society deftly mobilizes social-defense strategies in violation of traditional constitutional safeguards. In the case of youth, individuals are detained without bail, tried without a jury, and subjected to cruel and unusual punishment.[4]

That thousands of people continue to be victims of a humanitarian folly is attributed to two related developments. The first is the adoption by the proponents of the therapeutic state of what might be considered a criminal justice version of the philosophy of "infantile liberalism."[5] The second, and intellectual offspring of the first, is the professional mystification of social defense activities that defy scientific evaluation and public scrutiny.

Writing in *The Public Interest*, Kristol observes that many of our liberals today respond to economic inequality with a kind of "infantile liberalism," which calls for permanent reform. For example, he cites social critics who continually and vigilantly redefine poverty so that 20 percent of the nation's population is always "poor." However, he correctly notes that this definition of poverty is a function of ideology, not of sociology or economics or social science. For this group, objective analysis of a social condition is not necessary. Reality is predetermined. Of such critics, Kristol concludes:

> One usually concedes the sincerity of their moral passion while questioning the efficacy of their proposals. This is reasonable enough, most of the time. *But when that moral passion becomes intellectually petrified into a specified ideology, this sincerity can become transformed into a peculiar kind of fanaticism.* At that point, the purpose of reform becomes, not a change of condition which will satisfy the ostensible need, but rather the creation of circumstances which will legitimize in perpetuity the reforming passion itself [italics added].[6]

That juvenile justice is a casualty of "infantile liberalism" can be measured in the fanatic employment of unproven treatment techniques against captive clients by a professional correctional community petrified into the ideology of rehabilitation. In addition, it is seen in their undaunted commitment to decriminalization of juvenile crime and support of the indeterminate sentence. What was at the time a reasonable reaction to overly primitive nineteenth-century penal policy has become a "permanent revolution."

It is a reform that continues to grow in magnitude while covering its movements in the specialized language of rehabilitation and treatment. The remedies have run the gamut, ranging from repentance in solitude to guided group interaction. Other cures include reality therapy, transactional analysis, psychiatric casework, and, more recently, psychological counseling according to personality characteristics. More often than not, these so-called remedies are conducted in a custodial atmosphere by inexperienced apprentices; frequently the destiny of an entire cottage population is given to an enthusiastic practitioner for experimentation. In this instance, release is arbitrarily determined by the experimenter. Thus, it is not uncommon for two youngsters from the same town, incarcerated on the identical offense, to receive sentences which vary over a year. That such disparities go unnoticed or are rejected out of hand illustrates the degree to which the juvenile-justice community has become petrified into an ideology of experimentation far removed from the goals of justice, crime control, and public safety.

History has taught us that when ideology is transformed into unharnessed fanaticism, behavior is shrouded in mystique and the means become the end.

In this context, the principals view research as subversive activity and relegate communication of public business to contrived utterances of agency press agents. In addition there is the underutilization of available accountability technology, e.g., computer, or use of scientific evaluation. Finally, we may envisage the situation in which the "cure"—rehabilitation—

divests itself of the responsibility of dealing with the "disease"—juvenile crime. This brings us to the purpose of this undertaking.

Today, public policy governing juvenile crime is guided more by unproven "treatment" theories—petrified ideology— than a democratic assessment of what constitutes fair and just punishment. Therefore, any fundamental structural change in the juvenile justice system must evolve from an analysis aimed at exposing and dismantling the therapeutic state. To achieve these objectives—and proceed toward sound and constructive policy formulation—we must first understand the varied strategies of juvenile-crime control, its theoretical assumptions, and its impact on offenders and the public. From a practical point of view, it is no less significant, *if in the examination, we discover that our remedy for controlling delinquency functions as a counterdeterrent to crime.* It is the above perspective and thesis that I intend to show in this investigation. The book is divided into two parts.

Part I presents the theory and results of current juvenile sentencing and parole practices, including the social effects of the "revolving door" and "prisonization." Chapter 1 describes the foundations of counterdeterrence embodied in current public policy and its related negative social consequences in the areas of sentencing, correctional resource utilization, and official and "hidden" juvenile crime rate.

Chapters 2 and 3 identify and test the major theories of juvenile sentencing and classification. A statistical analysis of institution length of stay from data collected in a 1974 national survey is presented, including the findings of a two-year longitudinal study of juvenile offenders committed to institutions in a large Midwestern state.

Chapter 4 discusses the concept of the "revolving door" and its relationship to "individualized treatment." Release patterns of state juvenile institutions by offender characteristics are examined. This section also projects the long-term effect of probation subsidy programs and new monies on the size and composition of juvenile facilities.

Chapter 5 examines the purpose and nature of juvenile parole. Length of community supervision and outcome data are analyzed as well as the effects of parole on juvenile sentencing.

Part II focuses on significant social-policy issues, juvenile justice reform, and strategies of decriminalization. Chapter 6 explores the receptivity of training-school superintendents toward a "fixed" sentence.

Chapters 7 and 8 review the development of PINS (persons in need of supervision) legislation and the issue of coercive versus voluntary treatment. Dilemmas of decriminalization of juvenile law are introduced as well as actual "ideal type" community-based and institutional rehabilitation models.

Chapter 9 summarizes and discusses the findings with regard to juvenile sentencing, parole procedure, official attitudes toward definite sentences, the revolving door, decriminalization, and alternative models to coercive treatment. The final portion concentrates on social-policy implications of the major findings. It offers specific alternatives to combat the policies of counterdeterrence and abuses of the juvenile justice system.

ACKNOWLEDGMENTS

Many people directly and indirectly assisted me in the preparation of this report. I offer special thanks to Professor Leslie T. Wilkins, who graciously took time off from his busy schedule to review this material and write an introduction. His concern and inquiry into the inequities of the indeterminate sentence was a source of inspiration. Professor Fred Cohen, also of the State University of New York at Albany, was encouraging of this investigation. Direct assistance is acknowledged from a friend and colleague, D. Keith Nichols, Director of Administrative Services, Franklin Sheriff's Department, Columbus, Ohio, who coined the phrase, *child-welfare effect*, and helped write Chapter 4. With regard to typing, organization of the manuscript, and library research, I wish to thank Ms. Elaine Maney, secretary, Mrs. Lesley M. Schneider and Tom Browne, students, University of Maryland, Institute of Criminal Justice and Criminology. Looking back, I must recognize those outstanding mentors and practitioners who contributed to my professional development: Professors John H. Behling and Samuel Daykin, Ohio State University. I appreciate the guidance of University of Chicago's Professors Donnell Pappenfort and Irving Spergel. For a better understanding of social policy, I thank William B. Cannon, Vice President, Business and Finance, University of Chicago. In the community I have been privileged to know and work with outstanding grassroots organizers Ron and Lyn Lofstrom, cofounders of the Long Beach Free Clinic, and Jerry Grenna, director of the Long Beach Youth Action Commission. I am no less grateful to Samuel Ostroff of the Los Angeles County Probation Department; and Virgil Clark, Richard Simonetti, and other staff at Vernon Kilpatrick School for Boys, who made my unique experience in that setting possible. Their dedication, vision, imagination, and leadership in residential child care continue to be unparalleled in the public sector. Finally, to my wife Carol and daughters Heather and Shelley, I express a special sense of gratitude for the patience, moral support, and understanding for time not spent with them.

I

The Roots of Counterdeterrence:
Sentencing Disparity,
Parole Supervision,
and Prisonization

1
YOUTH AND CRIME: THE SOCIAL CONSEQUENCES OF COUNTERDETERRENCE

> When we cease to consider what the criminal deserves and consider only what will cure him, we have tacitly removed him from the sphere of justice altogether; instead of a person, a subject of rights, we now have a mere object, a patient, a "case."
>
> C. S. Lewis*

Paramount to the promotion of social order in a democratic society plagued with a soaring crime rate is an understanding of the principle of justice and its application in deterring crime and punishing offenders. In the past, social policy and strategies aimed at reducing crime rarely have taken into consideration the relationship between the youthful offender and punitive sanction or the threat of punishment. Historically, these dimensions have been ignored or seriously distorted to accommodate the needs of the "helping" professions and their ideological allies who inherited, and for the most part, continue to support the indeterminate sentence and its related assumptions of rehabilitation. Before describing these distortions and negative consequences of present social policy, it is appropriate to discuss the magnitude of juvenile crime in America and the foundations of counterdeterrence.

---

*C. S. Lewis, "The Humanitarian Theory of Punishment," *Crime and Justice* Vol. 2, (ed.) Leon Radzinowicz and Marvin Wolfgang, Basic Books, 1971, p. 44.

Youth and Crime

Crime is more and more a young man's profession. Over half of the seven million persons arrested each year are under age 25. In 1960, youth under 18 represented only 14 percent of the total arrests. In 1967, this figure jumped to 24 percent. Today, this group makes up 26 percent of the total arrests.[1] According to the *Uniform Crime Report,* young offenders are arrested more frequently than other age groups. Offenders under 20 were arrested every three months. This compares with an arrest every six months for 20-24 years and 22 months for older groups. While the rise in young arrests can be partially accounted for by the nearly 50 percent increase in the youth population, the rate of increase of youth involvement in serious crime cannot. Between 1960 and 1972, youth under 18 arrested on criminal homicide and robberies increased 259 and 263 percent respectively. Aggravated assault jumped 179 percent. Larceny and forcible rape doubled.[2]

In 1973, "of all persons arrested for robbery, 34 percent were under the age of 18."[3] Young persons under 18 accounted for 54 percent of all arrests for burglary that year.[4] From 1968 to 1973, arrests for aggravated assault have increased 42 percent for this age group.[5] In one state (Ohio), juvenile commitments more than tripled between 1964 and 1973 on FBI index crimes against the person.[6] But conventional crime reports still only show that 3 percent of the entire juvenile population under 18 is processed by the police and juvenile courts.[7] This figure merely represents "official" reported statistics. Using self-reporting data, we find that the percentage of young people engaging in felonious activity is staggering.

Hidden Delinquency

A 1972 statewide scientific survey[8] of 3,100 Illinois youth age 14 through 18 indicated that deviant behavior among adolescents is commonplace and that serious criminal behavior is significantly underreported. For example, 47 percent of the sample admitted having truanted from school. Forty-six percent stated that they got drunk. An estimated 418,000, or 56 percent of 14- to 18-year-old population in Illinois, reported keeping or using stolen goods. Thirteen percent admitted committing a breaking-and-entering. In regard to serious index crimes, 136,000 or 13 percent stated they have strong-armed. A higher 16 and 25 percent reported using or carrying a weapon. An estimated quarter of a million (22 percent) used marijuana and 5 percent reported selling drugs.[9]

Surprisingly, the researchers found little difference in social characteristics and delinquency involvement. With the exception of acts of personal violence where blacks report a high incidence of involvement, and auto violation where white adolescents have a distinct edge, the overall incidence of delinquency is similar for both races.[10] Girls engaged in less serious property crimes (shoplifting and petty theft) but broke the law as much as boys. Where parental education and father's job are used as social-status indicators, no major differences were observed. In reference to community background, the survey concluded: "Youngsters in Illinois reported generally similar levels of delinquency involvement whether they were interviewed on farms, or in towns, suburbs, or small or large cities."[11]

Therefore, using official and self-reporting indices, it appears that we can continue to expect more youth to enter the criminal justice system and for more serious crime against society. To what factors do we attribute these grim statistics?

Genesis of Illegitimacy

"The juvenile court is . . . the product of paternal error and maternal generosity, which is not an unusual genesis of illegitimacy."[12] This observation by Morris and Hawkins best explains the current relationship of youth to the criminal justice system.

> The juvenile court emerged from what was a legal misinterpretation of the parens patriae concept. This concept was developed for quite different purposes—property and wardship—and had nothing to do with what juvenile courts do now . . . with the quasi-legal concepts of parens patriae to brace it, this assumption of power blended well

with the earlier humanitarian tradition in the churches and other charitable organizations regarding child care and child-saving.[13]

The child savers were determined to make the juvenile court an instrument of "benevolent" intervention. The delinquent child would be "saved" rather than "punished." Nearly three-quarters of a century later, a Presidential Commission concluded that few children are saved. Punishment was not addressed. In the interest of the child and society, the commission recommended that troubled youth be diverted from the juvenile justice system to community-based rehabilitation programs.[14] Although laudable, this solution ignored the crux of the issue: the juvenile offender is left out of the criminal justice system.

Upon breaking the law, youth are consigned to a special category—delinquent. Because of age, potential delinquents and delinquents are removed from the policies and constraints of threatened punitive sanctions. The gravity of the act normally associated with crimes like armed robbery, homicide, and assault is nullified by age. Consequently, potential youthful offenders and delinquents perceive little relationship between antisocial acts and punitive sanctions. Given their immunity status, they literally do not know where they stand with the law if they engage in a prohibited act. What youth may realize is that whatever the social-control measure imposed will be governed by the philosophy of the indeterminate sentence, a principle that is in theory and application opposed to punishment, deterrence, and justice.

The indeterminate sentence will not punish because this smacks of retribution and presupposes rational behavior. Having established that juveniles, because of age, are incapable of free choice, we attribute their transgressions to psychological illness or socioeconomic deprivation. Since everyone agrees that it is unchristian to punish the "ill" and the deprived, we elected the term *treatment*. But, having failed to find an antidote to crime and delinquency, we are compelled to continue indefinitely our search for a cure.

Subjected to a medical model of correctional rehabilitation, the delinquent is cast into the therapeutic state. After adjudication, his commitment offense will be buried in the lexicon of psychosocial impressions and recommendations that neither he, the victim, nor the public understands. Whatever positive function punishment or the threat of punitive sanctions has on deterring criminal behavior is forfeited to "humanitarianism." In conflict with the concept of "maternal generosity" and the unitary definition of delinquency, punishment for deterrence purposes is discarded as barbarism. Subsequently, the benefits of both general and punitive prevention are denied to youth.

Sentencing and Counterdeterrence

Zemring states "the theory of simple deterrence is that threats can reduce crime by causing a change of heart, induced by the unpleasantness of the specific consequences threatened."[15] General punitive prevention according to Lejins is traditionally connected to a German jurist, Anselm Feurbach, "who saw a prevention factor in a potential offender's awareness of the threat of punishment or of the application of punishment to another offender."[16] General punitive prevention applies to the general adult population and is claimed to be the most important function of criminal law.

> In the context of motives to commit or not commit the prohibited act, the presence of awareness of this threat of punishment may presumably sway the balance in favor of abstaining from prohibited action.[17]

General punitive prevention is reflected in our criminal codes and local ordinances. Violations and penalties may range from a $5 fine for double-parking to a ten-year prison term for armed robbery. Theoretically, the threatened punishment is linked to the gravity of the crime. A person will be more discouraged to double-park if faced with a $100 than a $25 fine. But this is not true for bank robbers. Here a fine is considered an insufficient deterrent or lacking in disincentive to steal. Neither would it be considered just deserts in the eyes of society.

Tullock observed that deterrence is analogous to the price

system. If the "price" is too high, we will avoid the prohibited act, conversely, if the cost is too low, there may be incentive to engage in illegal acts. An important point to remember is that general punitive prevention is predicated on rational behavior and egalitarian application of negative sanctions.[18]

In contrast to general punitive prevention, which applies to potential criminals, special punitive prevention measures are actions taken against persons already convicted of crime. A judge may impose a harsh sentence on a law professor caught smoking pot to "teach him a lesson." Supposedly the offender will "think twice" before repeating the act. While sanctions vary according to community norms and individual judges, special punitive prevention is also related to seriousness of the violation.

In this context, any notion of deterring juvenile crime is lost to both the individual being punished and the potential offender. For deterrence to exist, the threatened audience must be aware of the consequences of engaging in prohibited behavior.[19] In addition there must be significant variation in punishment and these differences should correspond to the seriousness of the deviant act. However, as we will discover in the following chapters, sentencing for juveniles is more a function of the personality of the institution than the individual characteristics of the offender. Statistically this means that each institution imposes a "fixed" sentence unrelated to committing offense. A youth committed on an FBI index crime against the person will receive a similar sentence as the property offender and the runaway placed in the same institution.

Because the sentence is determined by the institution and not the law, no warning signals exist for the public (general deterrence) to discourage lawbreaking. To those already locked up, the threat of punishment (special deterrence) is compromised due to undifferentiated release practices. We may conclude that the indeterminate sentence in its present form functions as a counterdeterrent to crime because the hard-core offender perceives himself being punished the same as minor offenders. Conversely the minor law violator will see himself having nothing more to lose if he engages in more serious criminal acts.

Youth and Justice

The most negative social consequences of *parens patriae* and the indeterminate sentence is the repudiation of justice for the nation's youth. Under the banner of humanitarianism, solitary confinement is referred to as "intensive treatment." Parole is denied because of a "negative attitude." Humane and esoteric words displace the symbols of cruelty and deprivation. Because officials say they are doing good, no limits are set; vindictiveness and forgiveness by discretion is operationalized. Moreover, justice assumes a public review of actions taken by the government against all citizens, including lawbreakers. It allows open discussion of what constitutes severe or lenient penal sanctions. But such a dialogue is near impossible when institutions are permitted to report on themselves and define punishment as treatment. Finally, justice totally rejects the principle of delegating our most valuable possession—personal freedom—to a class of professional elites. As a group, institutional administrators are more concerned about managing stability and survival than promoting justice or crime control.

In this regard, given fluctuating commitment rates, the indeterminate sentence is a godsend. When population pressure is high, it permits administrators to release inmates indiscriminately. If there is minimal demand for beds, the indeterminate sentence will allow institutional staff to extend stay to assure maximum occupancy. This policy constitutes a built-in survival mechanism for institutions and related vested interest. The ultimate irrationality of this policy is seen in the unrelatedness between institution utilization and crime rate.

Institutional Utilization and Crime Rate

California has a relatively low rate of youth institutionalization but it ranks first in crime rate, whereas Ohio's institutionalization rate is similar but its crime rate is well below the national average. More disturbing is the observation that smaller youth-populated states with typically low crime rates have the highest rate of youth institutionalization.[20]

The above phenomenon is not uncommon in the health field. Roemer found that given the condition of prepaid health insurance, hospital utilization will increase but in no direct proportion to the rate of illness in the community.[21] A similar development is observed in patterns of hospital stay among post-Medicare patients. After passage of Medicare legislation (1965), hospital admission rates and average length of stay significantly increased.[22] Like the health field, additional funding in juvenile corrections is more often associated with new institution construction, longer sentences, and higher commitment rates. Whether these strategies curb crime or focus on the criminal population is coincidental. Over a quarter of the nation's juvenile correctional resources is expended on youth whose only offense is age. In some states, the bulk of resources is devoted to controlling status offenders (see Chapter 2).

Thus, the inevitable consequences of the policy of counterdeterrence or diverting the delinquent from the criminal justice system to the therapeutic state are the following: 1) corrections staff camouflage punishment in 1984 "child-saving" language; 2) juvenile crime rate will continue to soar because of the counterdeterrent effect of the indeterminate sentence philosophy; 3) a disproportionate amount of crime-control resources is expended on youth who present no threat to the community, and; 4) there is no relationship between crime rate and rate of institutionalization.

To alter the policy of counterdeterrence and its related social consequences, we must be prepared to challenge the theoretical assumptions and application of the indeterminate sentence in juvenile sentencing, parole, and rehabilitation.

2
THE MYTH OF THE
INDETERMINATE SENTENCE

> Justice is the first virtue of social institu-
> tions, as truth is of systems of thought. A
> theory however elegant and economical
> must be rejected or revised if it is untrue;
> likewise laws and institutions no matter
> how efficient and well-arranged must be re-
> formed or abolished if they are unjust.
>
> John Rawls*

In spite of the landmark Gault decision seven years ago, 56,000 youth continue to remain prisoners of the therapeutic state.[1] While we observe a rejection of the principle of *parens patriae* in the adjudication process, at the same time we see it readily adopted and reinforced in the rehabilitation phase of the juvenile correctional system. In 1974, this condition appears in the use of bona fide diagnostic and classification systems, i.e., the Interpersonal Maturity Level and Quay index, in nearly 40 percent of the state juvenile correctional agencies. In addition, employment of various "treatment" modalities such as behavior modification, reality therapy, transactional analysis, and psychiatric casework, are on the increase. Like the founders of the juvenile family court system, the intent of such

---

*John Rawls, *A Theory of Justice* (Cambridge: Harvard University Press, 1971) p. 3.

programs is to "individualize" treatment and separate the offender from the offense.[2]

If the above is true, the degree to which delinquent youth experience individualized treatment should be reflected in the institutional length of stay. Like the convalescent period of hospitalized patients subject to different treatments, we would expect length of institutional stay of "delinquents" classified and diagnosed for different "treatments"—under the indeterminate sentence—to vary significantly.

To determine the influence of the indeterminate sentence on the lives of the nation's incarcerated youth, a survey of the factors related to length of institutional stay in 30 states was conducted by this researcher. The purpose of the study was two fold. First, the theoretical assumptions of sentencing were reviewed, and, secondly, it analyzed organizational and offender variables related to length of institutional stay.

Theoretical Assumptions of Sentencing

There are three basic modes of sentencing: 1) tariff or fixed—prescribes the number of days, months, or years the offender will spend for violating a given law; the release date is determined by the law; 2) minimum—provides for a minimum and possibly maximum length of time in confinement; release is determined by the law and correcting agency; and 3) indeterminate—provides no time guideline; release is determined by the correcting agency. There may also be a combination of the above.[3]

The first two categories generally apply to adults. They also attempt to operationalize a length of stay in proportion to the seriousness of the offense. Theoretically (see Table 1), the intended social-individual impact of the fixed and, to a lesser degree, the minimum sentence, is deterrence. Because of the fear of punishment, society and the previous offender will be deterred from engaging in a criminal act. Table 1 also shows that, of the three types, the fixed sentence offers the lowest impact of "individualization" or commitment to work more closely and singularly with offenders. As expected, the juvenile sentencing procedure,* in theory, has the lowest deterrence and highest individualization. What are the advantages and disadvantages of each of the above modes of sentencing? To what degree does practice depart from theory?[4]

Table 1

RELATIONSHIP BETWEEN MODE OF SENTENCING
AND SOCIAL-INDIVIDUAL IMPACT

Mode of Sentencing	Social-Individual Impact	
	Individualization	Deterrence
Tariff (fixed)	Low	High
Minimum	Medium	Medium
Indeterminate	High	Low

The Fixed Sentence

D. A. Thomas, lecturer in law at the London School of Economics, defines *tariff* (fixed) as a process by which the length of the sentence is calculated, and where the primary decision is not in favor of an individualized measure.[5] Thomas also observed:

> It is . . . incorrect to speak of the tariff as a single entity, a continuous whole; there is in effect a series of separate and independent tariffs, each providing a pattern of sentences for a particular area of criminal behavior based on the fact situation most commonly found within that particular context.
>
> . . . This process is governed primarily by concepts of proportion, the relative seriousness of the offense or an instance of its kind, and arguments based on deterrence are not permitted to override this factor.[6]

In dealing with the fixed sentence for juveniles, two current systems are observed. In England, the court will either sentence a youth to a fixed period of borstal training according to the seriousness of the offense or an indeterminate sentence

---

*In actuality, juveniles are subject to a "relative" indeterminate sentence because most states will discharge them at age 21. One state (California, for example) retains juvenile jurisdiction until age 25.

on the basis of his character. The major consideration on the type of sentence is gravity of the offense and the deterrence factor:

> Where borstal training is imposed as a deterrent sentence, ... the sentence, in effect, is part of the tariff and is governed by tariff principles, the chief principle being that the sentence must not be excessive in relation to the offense.[7]

In Israel, a modified fixed sentence for juveniles is employed. After sentencing to an institution, the sentence is suspended for first-time offenders. Although the sentence is not correlated to the offense itself, it is linked directly to the number of times the offense is committed. In this instance, the focus is on the second offender.[8]

Minimum Sentence

Theoretically, the minimum sentence appears as a compromise between deterrence and individualization. By imposing a minimum term, the court conveys to society the seriousness of the violation while offering the correcting agency the opportunity to treat the offender individually in granting him parole. In practice, this procedure is viewed as impeding the equal process of justice and causing disparity with respect to sentences and length of sentences. In *Sentencing in a Rational Society*, Nigel Walker asserted:

> The higher the minimum, the weaker the non-deterrent arguments for it become, and the stronger the objection that it interferes with individualization; i.e., that it compels the system to deal more severely with some offenders than is necessary to correct them.[9]

Sol Rubin concurs, stating that "the minimum terms govern the parole eligibility. By the judge fixing a minimum term, he is, in effect, controlling parole."[10] Rubin found that in the United States adult penal system, "the principal effect of this ... idea ... has been an increase in the length of imprisonment."[11] He also concluded that little individualization was evidenced in the overcrowded prison population.

Thus, in regard to the fixed and minimum sentence, the critics opt for "a flexible tariff system to one based on a prescribed minimum."

The Indeterminate Sentence

The indeterminate sentence has been institutionalized in the American juvenile justice system. The theory behind the juvenile court is rooted in Social Welfare Philosophy rather than in corpus juris. It is theoretically engaged in determining the needs of the child and society rather than adjudicating criminal conduct.[12] The primary objectives are to insure certain meters of guidance to the child, along with the hope of rehabilitation. It must also provide adequate assurance of safety to society.[13]

In terms of institutionalization, most youth, especially first offenders, have no idea how long their length of stay or commitment to a correctional agency will be. Attorney Lois G. Forer observed: "Neither the state knows the duration of the commitment nor the standard of conduct required for release."[14]

Stuart King Jeffary attributed this condition to the fact that sentencing is more a social than a legal action.[15] He viewed the youth as reacting to a psychosocial situation rather than the law. According to Kahn, this atmosphere was promoted by the Children's Bureau at the turn of the century and continued by professional social workers:

> Through the 1940's and well into the 1950's [social welfare agency personnel] took an essentially clinical view of delinquency. Whatever the social context, they tended to think behavior must eventually be interpreted in psychological-motivational terms, and the roots of motivational dynamics were to be found in the parent-child relationship as seen as the product of psychosis, interpreted as either biologically or functionally determined; but much was in the realm of the primary behavior disorder to the neurosis. Conduct disorders in children were seen as "acting out" types of psychoneurosis.[16]

As shown in the diagram, juvenile sentencing has rejected

the notion of deterrence. "The purpose of the state statutes relating to the handling of youth offenders . . . is education."[17] Complying with the long-standing principle of *parens patriae*, the court, in essence, has assumed the role of the family. That is, it regarded itself and the juvenile laws as serving a benign rather than invidious purpose. Unfortunately, the facts suggest that these benevolent, if not lofty, expectations have not been realized.

To some scholars and practitioners, the juvenile court's insistence on the use of indeterminate sentencing has served only to dampen hope for the implementation of a truly equitable system of justice for juvenile offenders. Rubin asserts:

> The effect of indeterminate sentencing is to lengthen terms of imprisonment substantially, without regard to any compensatory positive results. The idea of returning the offender to society, fully rehabilitated, is lost, when the uncertainty of not knowing when and how long is hanging over them.[18]

In this regard, Irvin Ben Cooper maintained that "inappropriate sentencing plunges them into hatred, revolt, and self-destructive moral suicide."[19] It appears that neither individualization or deterrence was achieved in these practices. "Factors such as background . . . and the seriousness of conduct," according to Frank W. Miller, "are irrelevant in determining the length of period he may be held."[20] He found that the authorized period of confinement depends solely on the age of the child. "The younger the child, the longer the permitted period of detention."[21] Consistent with this view, Stephen Wizner stated that: "Children frequently remained in these institutions for years, for nothing more than truancy."[22]

This raises the issue of the function or purpose of institutional time itself.

Research and Length of Stay

Incredible as it may appear in the computer age, there is only scarce information on the effects of length of stay among the juvenile-offender population. This stems from two unrelated factors: 1) the first is the prior acceptance on the part of clinically oriented administrators that some treatment is going on; this is somewhat analogous to the time patients spend in the hospitals, which only recently came under scrutiny by health planners and the medical profession; and, 2) secondly, the record-keeping process and research effort of state juvenile correctional agencies have historically been primitive and not oriented toward accountability.

Empirically, the time an individual spends in an institution has been shown to make no difference or to increase chance of returning to jail.

The latter point was illustrated in 1966 in Eichman's study of matched offenders consisting of those released early due to the Supreme Court's *Gideon* decision:

> ... After two years 16 percent of the Gideon group [experimental] compared with 25 percent of the others [control—those who served full time], had been reconvicted. It would be unjustifiable to conclude that shortening period of incarceration in this way would always improve success rates; but not so unjustifiable to infer that at least it is unlikely to make them worse.[23]

The case against long stay is supported in Empey and Lubeck's findings reported in *The Silverlake Experiment*. In comparing the past recidivism rates of youth released early to a community (experimental group) project, against routine institutional stay, they found no difference.[24] However, they pointed out:

> It is significant that, while the community program was at least as effective as the more complex institutional programs, it completed its intervention in less than half the time [six vs. thirteen months].[25]

In terms of cost effectiveness, they concluded that a "significant pay off may have occurred."[26]

In a recent California study of institutionalized and non-institutionalized youth, it was shown that of those satisfactorily discharged, there was little difference in number, severity, or rate of offense committed on parole between these groups.[27]

The importance of examining length of stay cannot be dismissed. Street, Vinter, and Perrow stated:

> From a pure "efficiency" point of view, one could conceivably use data on an average length of stay as a measure of effectiveness, thinking of stay as the time it takes before the institution is ready to say the inmate is ready for release.[28]

Thus, institutional stay has been perceived as an important study variable by researchers. This brings us to the present operational definition of *institutional length of stay*.

Operational Definition of Institutional Length of Stay

There are many ways of examining length of institutional stay. Youth committed to state correctional agencies often pass through numerous local and state institutions before being paroled. For the purpose of this study, *stay* is defined as "the average period of confinement in the releasing institution." Multi-institutional time is excluded. Therefore, from the outset, it must be recognized that the figures in this study are deflated. Undoubtedly, the average total institutional-stay experience is greater. But, to achieve control over the variable "stay" in a national survey, a compromise was introduced.

A review of literature indicated that there exists only a sparse concern on the part of professionals and social scientists to examine length of stay in the correctional field. Heretofore, the most comprehensive analysis was made by Pappenfort and Kilpatrick of the University of Chicago.[29] They found considerable variation on stay between public and private institutions for delinquent children (see Table 2). Over 81 percent of the latter category detained youth one year or more. This compared to 14.5 and 8.2 percent for the state and local institutions respectively.[30]

Using their figures, the average length of stay in state institutions in 1966 was 9.6 months. According to the H.E.W. publication, *Statistics on Public Institutions for Delinquent Children 1970*, the average length of stay for these same type

Table 2

RELATIONSHIP BETWEEN TYPE OF INSTITUTION
AND LENGTH OF STAY BY PERCENT—1966

Average Length of Stay	State	Local	Private
Up to six months	20.3%	23.0%	.8%
Six months to one year	65.2%	68.8%	17.9%
Over one year	14.5%	8.2%	81.3%
Total	100%	100%	100%

SOURCE: Donnell M. Pappenfort & Dee Morgan Kilpatrick, A Census of Children's Residential Institutions in the United States, Puerto Rico, and the Virgin Islands: 1966 (Chicago: University of Chicago, The School of Social Administration, Vol. 3; 1970), p. 29.

facilities in 1970 was 8.8 months. [31] This study found that the average stay in 1973 in state juvenile institutions in 30 reporting states was 8.6 months. This indicated a greater decrease in average institutional stay between 1966 and 1970 (.8 months) than during the three-year period between 1970 and 1973 (.2 months).

The distribution of stay for 1973 is presented in Table 3. Of the 30 reporting states, only four—Connecticut, Illinois, Louisiana, and Wyoming—failed to give length of average institutional stay. Table 3 shows that of those that reported stay, Alabama and Texas confined youth the longest, and Kentucky and Idaho the shortest.

To ascertain the effect of organizational factors on stay, a three-way analysis of variance was employed. In this case, the institution size (average daily population), mode of classification, and parole board status were treated as the independent variables and length of stay as the dependent variable. Before presenting these findings, we will examine the main effect of important organizational variables on stay when tested independently.

Institution Size and Stay

In the 1974 reporting population of 30 states (see Figure 1), large institutions (100 and above average daily population)

Table 3

AVERAGE STATE INSTITUTIONAL STAY[a]
IN RANK ORDER—1973
BY AVERAGE MONTHS

STATE	STAY	STATE	STAY	STATE	STAY
Alabama	14.0	Michigan	9.0	New York	7.3
Texas	13.1	Arkansas	8.9	North Carolina	7.2
New Jersey	12.8	Wisconsin	8.4	Maryland	7.1
Indiana	12.0	Ohio	8.1	Tennessee	7.0
Alaska	10.8	Colorado	8.0	Arizona	6.0
California	10.6	South Carolina	8.0	Hawaii	6.0
Utah	10.5	Vermont	8.0	New Mexico	5.7
Florida	9.1	Iowa	7.3	Kentucky	5.5
Maine	9.0			Idaho	5.0

[a]No "stay" data on four reporting states; excludes multi-institutional stay
SOURCE: Ohio Youth Commission, Division of Research, Planning & Development, April, 1974.

were associated with longer stay. Compared to small institutions with an average stay of 8.4 months, large institutions showed 9.5 months. However, this finding was not found statistically significant (see Summary Table A, Appendix).

Testing the main effect of classification systems on institutional stay, it was found that institutions using the Interpersonal Maturity Level (I-Level), Quay, or a combination thereof confined youth significantly longer (9.8 months) than those employing the traditional APA or other (8.2 months). This difference was statistically significant at the less than .005 level. Surprisingly, there was no difference between parole board and staff-initiated institutional release. Both release the residents near the ninth month of confinement.

To determine if these relationships will change when introducing a third variable, a test of interaction was used. That is, the two independent variables, institution size and parole board status, will be treated as categorical variables and the dependent variable, stay, as metric data. Figure 1 demonstrates a slight, but nonsignificant interaction effect. We observe that, given the condition of small institutional size, the use of parole boards to determine release reduces average stay by almost one month. Whereas, given the condition of large

Figure 1

INTERACTION OF RELEASE METHOD
AND INSTITUTIONAL SIZE

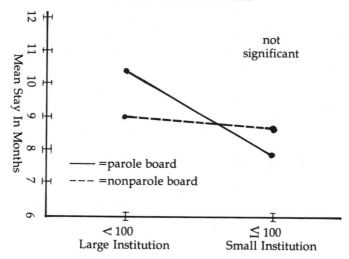

institution size, the application of parole boards is related to longer stay.

A similar pattern was observed when testing the interaction between mode of release and type of classification system on stay. Figure 2 shows that, given the condition of I-Level/Quay classification system, parole board institutions (10.4 months) have nearly a month longer stay than nonparole board or institution staff-authorized release (9.3 months). APA and other traditional classification type institutions were seen as generally releasing residents sooner than I-Level/Quay type institutions. But given the use of parole boards, institutional stay was considerably less (6.8 months) than nonparole institutions (8.5 months). However, these differences were not found statistically significant.

Figure 3 shows that there was minimal difference on stay between institution size and I-Level/Quay classification systems. Both averaged nearly 10 months. The traditional

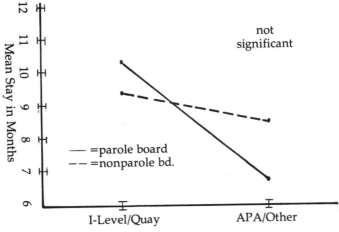

Figure 2
INTERACTION OF RELEASE METHOD
AND CLASSIFICATION SYSTEM

not
significant

— =parole board
– – =nonparole bd.

I-Level/Quay   APA/Other

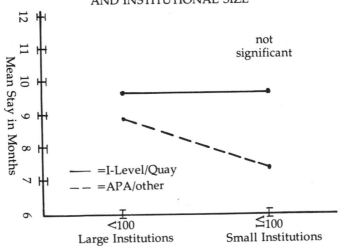

Figure 3
INTERACTION OF CLASSIFICATION SYSTEM
AND INSTITUTIONAL SIZE

not
significant

— =I-Level/Quay
– – =APA/other

<100   ≤100
Large Institutions   Small Institutions

20

classification type institutions (APA/other) show shorter length of stay and this is especially apparent in the small institutions that confine residents an average of 7.3 months. However, these differences are not statistically significant.

To access the interaction effect of organizational factors, we controlled all three independent variables. Figure 4-a shows that, given the condition of parole board and I-Level/Quay classification systems, large institutions detain youth over two months longer (11.3 months) than small facilities (9.1 months). This difference is considerably reduced in the APA/other category. This group generally confined youth a shorter period of time with little variation between large and small institutions.

Figure 4-b illustrates the degree to which this pattern changes in the nonparole board category. Given nonparole status institutions and utilization of I-Level/Quay classification systems, small institutions show longer length of stay (10.3 months) than large (9.0 months). Whereas, the opposite trend appears in the traditional APA/other classification-type facilities. Small institutions (8.1 months) release youth on the average almost one month sooner than large (9.0 months). Remarkably, little difference on stay was observed between I-Level/Quay and APA/other classification systems in institutions that did not have a parole board overseeing release. But upon examining the above interactional relationships, none of these differences were found statistically significant.

A more detailed analysis is made possible by presenting these findings in a two-by-two-by-two table.

Table 4 shows the interaction effect of the three independent variables on institution stay. To better understand these interactional relationships, it is necessary to make three sets of comparisons. First, we must compare each cell in the parole board category with the corresponding cell in the nonparole board category. Second, we must compare each cell in the I-Level/Quay columns with the corresponding cell in the APA/Other columns, and each cell in the large institution row(s) with the corresponding cell in the small institution row(s).

Figure 4

INTERACTION OF RELEASE METHOD,
INSTITUTIONAL SIZE, AND CLASSIFICATION SYSTEM

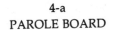

PAROLE BOARD

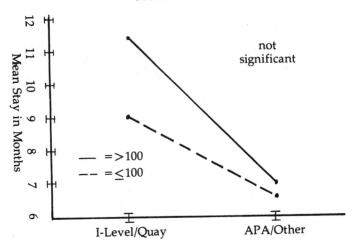

4-b

NO PAROLE BOARD

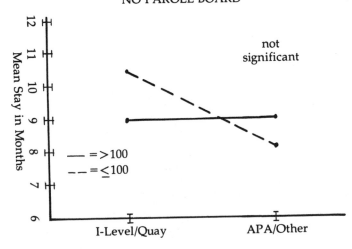

Table 4

INTERACTION OF RELEASE METHOD, INSTITUTIONAL
SIZE, AND CLASSIFICATION SYSTEM—
113 INSTITUTIONS—1973[a]

| Institution | Parole Board | | Nonparole Board | |
	I-Level/Quay	APA/Other	I-Level/Quay	APA/Other
Large	11.3 (A) months N=10	7.1 (B) N=3	9.0 (a) N=19	9.0 (b) N=26
Small	9.1 (C) N=7	6.7 (D) N=8	10.3 (c) N=10	8.1 (d) N=30

[a]Excludes institutions that did not report on all four variables

Making these comparisons results in the following figure.

Figure 5

Parole		Nonparole	diff.	Large Inst.		Small Inst.	diff.	I-Level/ Quay		APA/ Other	diff.
A	>	a	2.3	A	>	C	2.2	A	>	B	4.2
B	<	b	1.9	B	>	D	.4	C	>	D	2.4
C	<	c	1.2	a	<	c	1.3	a	=	b	0
D	<	d	1.4	b	>	d	.9	c	>	d	2.2

The difference in average months in stay appears in the "diff." column. The results show that the greatest difference (4.2 months) occurred between large I-Level/Quay and APA/Other institutions governed by a parole board. *Interaction occurs, but it is largely explained by large institutions with I-Level/Quay classification systems in the parole board category* (see cell A, Table 4). These institutions have a much higher mean stay (11.3 months) than would be expected due to main effect alone. In addition, this cell would be the main contributor to the interaction observed between classification systems and release method (see Figure 2). Finally, while the presence of a parole board did not significantly affect length of institutional stay (only one of four categories exceeded two months variation), the method of release appeared to be an important interactive variable. Except in large institutions associated with I-Level or Quay, parole boards consistently release youth sooner than nonparole-type facilities. We also observe that there is less variation within the nonparole board, than parole board categories.

The above data suggests that parole boards may be more

sensitive to offender-related variables than institution staff or administrative staff (nonparole board) responsible for approving release. This will become more apparent when we examine the relationship between offender characteristics and stay. However, only one of these relationships—I-Level/Quay related to longer stay—was sustained in a test of statistical significance. None of the interaction relationships were found statistically significant. Also, the fact that minimal variation was demonstrated in the nonparole board category that governs over 80 percent of the state institutions in the United States, supports the notion that a uniform, as opposed to differentiated, pattern of release is at work in the juvenile justice system. The report will now focus on the effect of offender characteristics on stay.

Offender Characteristics and Stay

Only 5 of 30 reporting states elected or were able to report institutional stay by offender characteristics. These data are presented in Table 5. Only one state, California, significantly differentiated between FBI index crimes and status offenses in regard to institutional stay. California was also the only state in this group governed by a juvenile parole board. Variation in stay was particularly evident in the index crimes against the person. Compared to these offenders who averaged 17.8 months, California status offenders were confined for an average period of 11.2 months. Three of the five states, Idaho, Arkansas, and Ohio, show less than one-month variation between FBI index and status offenses.

In view that the vast majority (84 percent) of reporting states did not concern themselves with the relationship between offense and incarceration time, and the five that did show minimal differentiation suggest that offense at commitment is a poor predictor of stay. The fact that minimal variation on stay by offense was found within states further supports the conclusion that arbitrary sentencing practices is "par for the course" in the juvenile justice system. It also indicates that organizational factors within states may be more im-

Table 5

RELATIONSHIP BETWEEN INSTITUTIONAL STAY[a]
AND COMMITTING OFFENSES BY MONTHS—
FIVE STATES (1973)

Type of Offense	N.C.	Idaho[b]	Calif.[c]	Ark.	Ohio
FBI Index Crime:					
Against Person	8.2 (months) —		17.8	10.5	8.5
Against Property	7.8	7.1	10.3	7.2	8.0
Total	8.0	7.1	14.1	8.6	8.3
Status	5.4	8.1	11.2	8.5	8.3

[a]Stay—time spent in releasing institution; excludes multi-institutional placements and diagnostic time if appropriate
[b]No data on crimes against person
[c]Use parole board

portant in determining stay than offender characteristics. This observation will become more evident in the next chapter when we analyze the juvenile sentencing practices of an individual state.

The Myth of the Indeterminate Sentence

These findings strongly contradict the theoretical assumptions of the indeterminate sentence. A pattern of uniformity rather than differential treatment emerged in institutional stay of youth committed to state correctional agencies. Quantitatively, only one of eight organizational hypotheses was supported by a test of statistical significance. Even in the former (I-Level/Quay related to longer stay), the variation was considerably reduced when other organizational variables were introduced. The therapeutic state also failed to "individualize" according to committing offense. Status offenders and youth charged on felony index crimes received a similar sentence.

The postadjudication phase of the juvenile justice system appears as irrational and arbitrary in meeting the needs of troubled youth and the community as the pre-Gault family court. The evidence suggests that delinquent youth are "processed" through the therapeutic state. If the indeterminate sentence is proven a myth, what possible rehabilitative objective or sense of fair play is achieved in the eyes of the offender? Committed to a sentence unrelated to offense at time of commitment, the offender perceives no relationship between his behavior and "treatment" or punishment. Furthermore, society is shortchanged because there is little official discrimination in the correctional component of the juvenile justice system between the dangerous and status offender. Where the former may legitimately pose a risk to the community, he may, in effect, receive a more lenient sentence, whereas the young status offender, subject to the stigma of criminalization, experiences no program payoff in terms of resolving his problem in the community. *Ironically, the net effect of the therapeutic state is to decriminalize the felony-index offender, while assigning a criminal role to the status violators.*

The absurdity of the present condition is dramatized in the fact that many citizens are justifiably afraid to walk the streets, while many of our juvenile institutions are incarcerating youth with histories of only runaways and school truancy. In the 1974 survey, 25 percent of the states' institutionalized delinquent population fell in the status-offender category.

Table 6

PERCENTAGE OF STATUS OFFENDERS IN 1973—
25 STATES

State	Percent	State	Percent	State	Percent
North Carolina	54	Louisiana	28	Indiana	15
Maryland	43	Connecticut	27	Iowa	15
Tennessee	43	Texas	26	Utah	13
Idaho	41	Maine	21	New Mexico	8
Arizona	37	Arkansas	20	California	6
Hawaii	36	Ohio	19	Alabama	0
Wyoming	34	Michigan	18	Alaska	0
New Jersey	33	Kentucky	16	Illinois	0
Florida	32			TOTAL STATE AVERAGE 25%	

The percent of status offenders ranged from a high of 54 percent in North Carolina to none reported in Alabama, Alaska, and Illinois (see Table 6). Five of the 30 reporting states: Colorado, New York, South Carolina, Vermont, and Wisconsin, did not differentiate between FBI index and status offenses. The state that had the highest proportion of status offenders (North Carolina—54%) showed the shortest average length of institution stay (5.4 months). The longest stay (11.2 months) was found in California (see Table 5), which showed the lowest proportion (6%) of status offenders. But nationally, it is difficult to posit a pattern with respect to institution population and sentencing. States with similar mean stays (Ohio—8.3 months, Arkansas—8.5 months, Arizona—8.1 months) varied significantly in percentage of status offenders.

The lack of relationship between offense at commitment and average length of stay of states' correctional institutions is an important finding. It suggests that the philosophy of the indeterminate sentence has created the conditions for establishing a juvenile sentencing structure impervious to the needs of incarcerated youth, values of justice, and concern for public safety. This observation will become more apparent when we examine the "revolving-door" phenomenon in Chapter 4.

3
A LONGITUDINAL STUDY OF JUVENILE INCARCERATION AND EFFECTS OF PRISONIZATION

> **A wholly treatment-oriented philosophy of punishment could make a strong case for no limitations on prison terms. If treatment really were the only value to be served by the sentencing of criminals, it perhaps would follow that so long as cure has not been effected detention should continue no matter what the offense. . . .**
> **American Bar Association—1967***

Many studies have shown the negative consequences of the indeterminate sentence.[1] However, most of the research has been confined to the adult correctional system. Nearly two decades ago, Rubin found that indeterminate sentencing resulted in longer imprisonment without any effect on rehabilitation.[2] Another point of criticism was the lack of uniformity in sentencing. Proposing a model sentencing code in its 1967 publication *Sentencing Alternatives and Procedures*, the American Bar Association observed:

> One of the most serious deficiencies in the manner by which sentences are now imposed is the existence of severe disparities in the disposition of comparably situated offenders. There is clearly a need for the adoption of technique which will introduce greater rationality into the sentencing process.[3]

---

*Sentencing Alternatives and Procedures (American Bar Association, 1967) p. 82.

According to the Council of Judges of the National Council of Crime and Delinquency, introducing a prescribed minimum sentence did not help.

> In its application the indeterminate sentence, heretofore the only legislative attempt to combat disparities, has increased rather than decreased it. The provision for a minimum term creates disparity of sentence by setting a mandatory term of incarceration. One defendant may receive a term of one to five years, another two to four, three to five, three to six and so on. . . .[4]

Such disparities were documented in a recent study by Scott in which he found that older offenders and males are punished more severely.[5] Also a correctional study group with the Academy of Contemporary Problems concluded:

> Evidence is accumulating that this system does not accomplish its objectives, does not play a significant part in the resocialization of the offender, and does not affect recidivism sufficiently for the effect to be statistically detectable. We advocate the discontinuance of indeterminate sentencing in favor of fixed maximum terms to be imposed by the court at the time of sentencing.[6]

Turning to the juvenile correctional system, the indeterminate sentence has received a prior acceptance as the alternative to the "fixed" sentence and the stigma of punishment associated with adult criminal codes.[7]

In regard to juvenile sentencing, research data on length of stay is scarce and relatively unobtainable. As described in the previous chapter, in 1966, Pappenfort and Kilpatrick found that private agencies detained delinquent children twice as long as public.[8] Also this investigation found that only 5 of 30 states recorded institutional stay by offender characteristics. To make a valid assessment of the effect of the indeterminate sentence in the juvenile justice system, a quantitative analysis of the relationship of offender and institutional factors to length of stay and recidivism is required. To conduct such an analysis, considerable control over the variables is necessary. This was achieved by using a computer to "track" subjects for a two-year period.

The Sample and Methodology

The sample consisted of a three-month cohort (686 cases) of youth committed to a Midwestern state's youth commission in 1972 (see Table 1). The youth were placed in nine large institutions or camps, including the diagnostic center, for a minimum of five months. Beyond this period, the state law gives the agency discretion to return youth to the community. Institution stay is defined as the number of consecutive days a youth was incarcerated in one or more institutions, including diagnostic time, before he was paroled to the community.

The average institutional stay was obtained by calculating the mean score in days between intake and release. Because the results showed a slight but tolerable skew and met the assumption of metric data, analysis of variance was employed. Where the number of cases appearing in cells was too limited to draw statistical inference, a descriptive analysis is offered.

The first section of the report will examine the total cohort's institution stay by offender-related variables. Sex, race, and age are straightforward. Offense was determined by classifying the committing offense into four categories: Type I refers to FBI-index crimes against person (gross felonies), i.e., murder, strong-arm or armed robbery, and rape; Type II includes FBI-index crimes against property (gross felonies), i.e., auto theft, grand larceny, and breaking and entering; Type III includes other felonies and gross misdemeanors, i.e., forgery, prostitution, possession or use of illegal drugs, purse snatching, and probation violation; and Type IV offenses encompass minor misdemeanors and status offenses, i.e., unruly, incorrigibility, truancy, and malicious mischief.

The next part will examine the relation of offender characteristics to stay controlling on institution assignment. The final section will analyze the effects of institution stay ("prisonization") on recidivism taking into account offender characteristics.

Social Characteristics and Stay

Examining the total distribution (see Table 1), the data showed the females were confined slightly longer (243 days) than males (225 days). The difference was statistically significant at the less than .05 level (T = 1.79, P = <.05). In terms of race, black males averaged seven days shorter stay than their white counterparts. Among females, blacks' stay was nearly a month longer (262 days) than whites' (236 days). This variation was statistically significant at the less than .05 level (T = 1.75, P = <.05).

Surprisingly, age was inversely related to average length

Table 1

SUMMARY OF INSTITUTION STAY
1972 THREE-MONTH COHORT—686 CASES

Independent Variable	N	Mean (days)	T/F Test	Sign.
SEX:				
Male	528	225 (days)		
Female	158	243	1.79	<.05
RACE:				
Male White	311	228		
Black	217	221		NS
Female White	113	236		
Black	45	262	1.75	<.05
AGE				
Male 10-14 yrs.	83	275		
15 yrs.	135	232		
16 yrs.	143	216		
17 and over	167	201	7.73	<.01
Female 10-14 yrs.	22	238		
15 yrs.	53	228		
16 yrs.	39	235		
17 and over	44	270		NS
OFFENSE[a]:				
Male: I	71	231		
II	216	222		
III	182	227		
IV	58	220		NS
Female: I	5	296		
II	7	270		
III	59	247		
IV	87	236		NS

[a]No data on 1 case

of total institution stay only in the male population (F = 7.73, P = <.01). We observed nearly a three-month difference between the average stay of the 10- to 14-year-old male group (275 days) and those 17 and over (201 days). The pattern was somewhat reversed for girls. The oldest category stayed a month longer (270 days) than the youngest (238 days). But these differences were not sustained in a test of significant difference.

In view that age and race appeared to affect length of stay in opposite directions in the male and female population, we tested these relationships controlling on race and committing offense.

Race and Offense

Table 2 shows that the pattern of black females associated with longer stay holds regardless of offense. The difference is particularly apparent in Type I and III offense categories. Female blacks who were committed for a crime against the person averaged over three months longer in the institution than their white counterparts. They were detained nearly a month longer for minor misdemeanors. There were too few cases to draw meaningful statistical inference but the pattern suggests that race is more important than offense in predicting stay in the female population. At the same time, offense appeared to influence stay for blacks but not for white female offenders.

Table 2

LENGTH OF STAY FOR MALES AND FEMALES
BY RACE AND OFFENSE

	Females		Males	
	N = 158		N = 527	
	White	Black	White	Black
I	253 (days)	350	246 (days)	226
II	259	299	226	217
III	234	262	236	213
IV	234	244	204	279

In regard to males, the findings showed that blacks on the average were released slightly sooner than whites except for Type IV (status offenses). In this category, blacks were detained two months (279 days) longer than whites (204 days). However, none of these differences were statistically significant. Thus, except for the least serious offender (Type IV), neither race or offense appeared to affect stay for males.

Age and Race

Controlling on age at time of commitment, the relationship between race and length of stay held for females but was inconclusive for males. Table 3 shows that the highest variation on stay for females is observed in the 10 to 14 age group. Compared to whites (218 days), black females' length of stay averaged 273 days. This difference was statistically significant at the less than .05 level (T = 2.0, P = <.05).

Table 3

LENGTH OF STAY OF MALES AND FEMALES
BY AGE AND RACE

	Females		Males	
	N = 157		N = 528	
	White	Black	White	Black
10-14 yrs.	218 (days)	273	251 (days)	310
15	227	235	246	208
16	229	253	219	212
17 & over	263	287	206	195

Among males, the same pattern held in the youngest age group. The average stay for 10- to 14-year-old blacks was two months longer (310 days) than whites (251 days). The difference was statistically significant (T = 1.92, P = <.05). The opposite direction was found in the 15-year-old group. Black males were released on the average a month (208 days) sooner than whites (246 days). This difference was also statistically significant (T = 2.00, P = <.05). In the older groups, blacks were released slightly sooner.

The above findings suggest that age, race, and offense are important variables in explaining length of institution stay.

Black females appeared to stay longer and this was particularly evident in the youngest and oldest categories and among offenders who were committed on a FBI-index crime against the person. In the male population, blacks experienced a shorter stay except in the least-serious-offense category. The same was true for the youngest age group of blacks. They showed the highest mean stay.

Age, Offense, and Stay

To determine the effect of age and offense on stay, a one-way analysis of variance was employed holding these variables constant. Due to limited number of cases in cells, this was not attempted in the female population.

Table 4

RELATIONSHIP BETWEEN AGE AND OFFENSE
ON STAY BY SEX—685 CASES

Age	Males Offense				Females Offense			
	I	II	III	IV	I	II	III	IV
10-14	320 (days)	289	256	260	336	—	220	242
15	231	208	265	227	172	363	242	203
16	211	230	201	215	321	106	218	243
17 & over	215	198	207	165	—	232	305	258

Table 4 illustrates the degree to which institution stay is a function of age and offense. The data on females shows that the 15-year-old property offender (Type II) experienced longer institutionalization than her older counterparts. This pattern changes in the less-serious-offender group (Type III & IV). The oldest youth are associated with longer stay. The shortest length of stay (106 days) was observed in the 16-year-old index crime (Type II) category. The longest stay (363 days) was observed in the 15-year-old index crime against property (Type II) group.

The findings on the male population show similar sentencing disparities. The longest stay (320 days) was observed in the 10- to 14-year-old Type I group. The shortest stay (165 days) was seen in the 17 and older Type IV status offense category. Compared to females, there was a more consistent pattern of detaining younger male offenders longer than their older counterparts regardless of the offense. For example, we found that the 10- to 14-year-olds committed on index crimes against the person were confined over three months longer than the two oldest categories for the same offense. These differences were found statistically significant (F = 2.32, P = <.01).

Comparing sex and length of stay, we found that younger (10 to 15 years) less-serious male offenders received longer sentences than their female counterparts. The opposite is true for the older groups. For index type offenses, males generally had a lower mean stay. That females showed a higher mean stay than males in the total population is explained in the fact that most serious (Type I and II) female offenders are confined substantially longer than males in this category. Also, the less-serious older female offenders had higher mean stay than their male equivalent.

The Institutional Factor

The analysis of the institutional effect on sentencing confirmed its importance as an intervening factor. On the whole, institutional assignment or releasing facility appeared more important in determining the duration of confinement than the offenders' social characteristics or committing offenses.

Table 5
SUMMARY OF TOTAL INSTITUTIONAL STAY
BY INSTITUTION AND AGE—158 FEMALES

Age	Institution	
	A	B
10-14	234 (days)	321
15	207	442
16	210	388
17 and over	239	440
Total	221	421

Female Institutions: Age, Race, and Offense

While the limited cases precluded statistical analysis of the female age distribution, Table 5 shows that there is considerably higher variation between institutions given the same age group than between age categories within any given institution. For example, 15-year-old girls stayed twice as long in B as in A facility.

In regard to race, black females tend to experience longer institutionalization. But this is explained by one institution (see Table 6). Blacks stayed a month longer than whites in institution A (T = 1.99, P = <.02). The opposite was found in institution B. Blacks were on the average released 25 days sooner, but this difference was not statistically significant.

Table 6

SUMMARY OF TOTAL INSTITUTIONAL STAY
BY INSTITUTION AND RACE—158 FEMALES

Race	Institution	
	A	B
White	211 (days)	429
Black	246	404

Table 7 shows the same pattern on offense and stay when controlling for institution. Females committed to B institution on a Type II offense (FBI-index crime against property) received three times (462 days) the sentence as their A counterparts (126 days). This disparity is true regardless of the offense and when comparing the mean stay of both institutions. Remarkably, the shortest sentence was associated with the most serious offense in "B" institutions, whereas A facility detained this group the longest.

Male Institutions: Age, Race, and Offense

Table 8 shows the distribution of length of stay of males by age and institution. As in the female population, there appears higher variation of stay for males between institutions' given age category than between age groups within an institution.

Table 7

SUMMARY OF TOTAL INSTITUTIONAL STAY
BY INSTITUTION AND OFFENSE—158 FEMALES

Offense	Institution	
	A	B
I	240 (days)	380
II	126	462
III	220	406
IV	226	444
Total	221	422

The highest variation (17 months) is observed between "A" and "B" institutions among 15-year-olds. A one-way analysis of variance showed that these variations were statistically significant (F = 13.26, P = <.01).

Table 8

SUMMARY OF TOTAL INSTITUTIONAL STAY
BY INSTITUTION AND AGE—528 MALES

Age	Institution					
	A	B	C	D	E	F
10-14	258 (days)	—	309	470	307	163
15	197	726	283	541	257	194
16	193	486	396	443	219	123
17 and over	189	487	—	—	186	171
Total	195	501	305	493	241	165

This data reaffirms the importance of age in determining length of stay. Most institutions detained younger offenders longer but these differences were less than between institutions given similar age groups or between institutions as a whole.

In regard to race, there was strong evidence of reverse discrimination in the releasing practices of male institutions. Table 9 shows that the majority of male institutions released blacks sooner than whites (F = 25.0, P = <.01). In only two facilities (C and F) were blacks detained longer than white offenders.

Examining the effect of institution and offense (see Table 10), the findings clearly showed that stay is a function of institutional assignment more than committing offense. Exclud-

Table 9

SUMMARY OF TOTAL INSTITUTIONAL STAY
BY INSTITUTION AND RACE—528 MALES

Race	Institution					
	A	B	C	D	E	Fa
White	198 (days)	534	253	499	242	155
Black	191	440	348	466	239	198
Total	195	501	305	493	241	165

aDiagnostic Center

ing the diagnostic center, difference in mean stay exceeded one year between institutions in three of the four offense categories. An analysis of variance indicated that these differences could be attributed to chance less than one of a hundred times $(F = 12.50, P = <.01)$. The greatest sentencing disparity (529 days) was observed between "A" and "B" institutions among status or Type IV offenders. *In four of six institutions, short stay is associated with the serious offense categories.*

Table 10

SUMMARY OF TOTAL INSTITUTIONAL STAY
BY INSTITUTION AND OFFENSE—528 MALES

Offense	Institution					
	A	B	C	D	E	Fa
I	191 (days)	416	347	562	215	150
II	194	557	310	478	241	135
III	200	374	289	483	249	210
IV	189	718	297	483	231	160
Total	195	501	305	493	241	165

aDiagnostic Center

The main effect of institutions on stay was also examined. These variations were sustained in a test of statistical significance $(F = 50.75, P = <.001)$.

Observations on "Treatment" Program and Stay

As expected, the male (B and D) and female (B) facilities that historically have been identified as "long-term treatment" institutions showed the highest mean stay. In terms of policy, assignment to these facilities was predicated on behavior perceived as "aggressive" or emotional problems unamenable to "open" or less structured "rehabilitation" programs. Many of these youth are transferred from "short-term" facilities subsequent to runaway or "poor institutional adjustment." Committing offense, as the above table demonstrates, plays an insignificant role in these decisions. If a home truant is assigned to these facilities, he will receive a significantly longer sentence than a violent offender who remains in a "short-term" placement. We will now examine the effects of institutionalization—"prisonization"—on rehabilitation.

Length of Stay and Prisonization

In 1940, Donald Clemmer theorized that inmates will conform to prison norms in direct proportion to times of incarceration.[9] "Prisonization" is also seen as possibly having a deteriorating effect on behavior that would in turn impede parole adjustment.[10] Research findings are mixed (see Chapter 2, page 26). The results of this investigation appear to support the "prisonization" hypothesis in that return status or parole violation was positively associated with longer institutional stay.

Girls who were returned experienced longer (228 days) institutionalization than those who were successfully discharged from parole (207 days). This pattern was demonstrated for both black and white youngsters (see Table 11) but was not found statistically significant.

Table 11

AVERAGE LENGTH OF STAY BY RETURN STATUS—
94 FEMALES

| Race | Return Status | |
	Returned	Discharged
White	224 (days)	199
Black	251	231
Total	228	207

The same trend was found among the male population (see Table 12). Average stay for returnees was 226 days. This compared to a mean stay of 189 days for those successfully discharged. Among males, the difference was statistically significant for the total distribution ($T = 2.80, P = <.01$) and when controlling on race ($T = 2.00, P = <.02; T = 2.20, P = <.02$).

Table 12

AVERAGE LENGTH OF STAY BY RETURN STATUS—
353 MALES

| Race | Return Status | |
	Returned	Discharged
White	228 (days)	192
Black	223	186
Total	226	189

This pattern held for the total population when controlling on offense and age in males and among females when taking offense into consideration (see Tables 13 and 14). It also held when controlling for institutional effect (In all eight facilities, longer stay was associated with return or recommitment). Due to the bias of transferring older youth to the adult authorities, 17 and older groups were eliminated. Because of limited number of cases in cells, no statistics test of significance was attempted. These findings are somewhat inconclusive but they merely reject the notion that deterrence is a function of institutionalization.

Table 13

STAY AND RETURN STATUS BY OFFENSE AND AGE—
225 MALES

| | Offense | | | |
| Age | Major I and II | | Minor III and IV | |
	Success	Fail	Success	Fail
10-14	205 (days)	328	295 (days)	253
15	176	179	167	253
16	202	209	173	211

Table 14

STAY AND RETURN STATUS BY OFFENSE—
50 FEMALES[a]

| | Offense | |
Return Status	Major I and II	Minor III and IV
Success	163 (days)	156 (days)
Fail	—[b]	226

[a]Due to no cases in some cells, age groups were combined
[b]No cases fell in this category

Any final interpretation of these findings would be incomplete if the salient alternative hypothesis was overlooked.

Review of the Decision-Making Hypothesis

These findings generate two hypotheses relative to institutional stay: the first hypothesis states that institutionalization experience per se has a deteriorating effect on parole outcome for those most subjected to it.

The second and alternative hypothesis states that the longer stay for returnees was a function of greater-risk inmates being held in the institution longer by the releasing authority (institution staff). In this situation, we would expect return status to be related to longer sentences because this group was purposely held back from release because they were viewed the most likely to violate parole. Such a thesis would be supported if we could show that each institution applied the indeterminate sentence in this direction and indeed predicted parole outcome of its offenders.

To determine the plausibility of this position, the investigator analyzed the effect of "prisonization," taking into account the institution. In this respect, the results in all eight institutions supported the alternative hypothesis: each institution confined returnees longer. To answer the other related question—the ability of staff to predict parole outcome—the researcher turned to another study. The fact that it was conducted in the same state in one of the institutions (B) examined in the present study obviously adds to its interpretation and validity.

To determine institution staff's ability to predict parole outcome, Dinitz and Miller classified offenders according to levels of community adjustment and asked the staff member instrumental in release recommendation and whom "the boy said knew him best," to predict parole outcome. In only 72 of 443 cases (16 percent) were the staff able to predict parole outcome. Of those offenders staff thought were "headed for serious trouble," less than half (48 percent) were reincarcerated; of those they predicted "will make pretty good adjustment" over 40 percent returned to the institution.[11]

Upon reviewing Dinitz's and Miller's results, Professor Harry Allen, Director, Program for the Study of Crime and Delinquency, the Ohio State University, observed:

> While the results of this study may not be conclusive . . . nevertheless they cast significant doubt on one assumption [release authority's ability to predict parole outcome] underlying the use of the indeterminate sentence.[12]

These findings cast considerable doubt on the alternative hypothesis. Therefore, while the present findings may not confirm the hypothesis of "prisonization" with certainty, it surely leans toward rejecting the notion that deterrence and rehabilitation are a function of institutionalization.

Conclusion

This study has presented an analysis of a three-month cohort of youth committed to a large Midwestern state correctional agency in 1972. The findings demonstrated that sentencing for juvenile offenders is determined more by the personality of the institution than the individual characteristics of the offender. While offender-related variables were found important determinant factors, variations in length of stay were reduced or disappeared when we controlled on institutional assignment. Black females were associated with longer stay in the total population. But when we controlled for institution assignment, we found that this was true only in the old—low cost per day—"custody-oriented" facility. In the high cost per day, newly constructed and long-term "treatment" institution, white females were confined significantly longer than blacks.

Among males there was also evidence of "reverse" discrimination in the more modern—high cost per day—institutions. It may be suggested that this pattern in sentencing is explained by offense at commitment. This argument is not supported. Like the findings in the total distribution (see Table 1, page 45), given race and institutional assignment, offense is a poor predictor of length of institutional stay (see Table B, Appendix, Chapter 3, page 158).

That the long-term "treatment-oriented" institutions consistently released blacks sooner, regardless of offense at commitment, may be attributed to a lower social (rehabilitation) investment in blacks. In State X, significant "reverse" discrimination in sentencing among males was associated with institutions that had a lower proportion of black residents (30 percent—"B", 20 percent—"D"). The percentage of blacks in shorter-stay "custody" facilities,* which showed either no significant difference in stay between races, or significant discrimination against blacks, ranged from a low 32 percent (E) to a high of 60 percent (C). In the female group, the racial composition in both A and B institutions was the same (30 percent black). But the latter, identified as a "treatment" program, detained whites, on the average, two months longer than blacks.

The conclusion that "reverse" discrimination in long-term "treatment-oriented" institutions is explained by a lower social investment in blacks is supported by Pappenfort's et al., national study: "Factors Accounting for Variation in Use of Public Institutions for Delinquent Children in the United States and in Expenditures for Their Care."[13] He found that "the relationship of percent nonwhite with expenditures is negative: the larger the percentage of nonwhites in the state, the smaller the investment of public money per capita in salaries and wages to man the institutions" (see Table 15).[14]

Pappenfort's analysis also showed statistical evidence that

---

*Although the mean stay of black residents in the largest "custody" male facility (A) was lower for the total population, this was explained by (black) Type III (misdemeanors) offenders. In offense categories I, II, and IV blacks were confined longer than whites (see appendix, page 158).

length of institutional stay was a function of average daily population of institutions.[15] This was consistent with the findings on State X. The average daily population of long-term residential "treatment" facilities was substantially lower than its short-term traditional "custody" institutions. The average daily population of State X's shortest stay (195 days) male institution (A) was 820. The longest average length of confinement (501 days), was associated with the institution (B) with an average daily population of 175 youth. For females, the long-

Table 15

REGRESSION OF PER CAPITA EXPENDITURES
ON SIX VARIABLES:

Expenditures For Health, Education, and Welfare; Percent of Adults with High School or Greater Education; Percent of Children Served by Voluntary Child Welfare Agencies; Per Capita Income; Percent Nonwhite; and Percent of Children in Broken Homes.

Independent Variable	Beta Coefficients	Multiple Correlation Coefficients
Per capita expenditures for health, education, and welfare	.290	
Percent of adults with high school or greater education	.385*	
Percent of children served by voluntary child welfare agencies	—.291*	
Per capita income	.299*	
Percent nonwhite	—.322*	
Percent of children in broken homes	.349	.763**
Level of significance: *P = .05 **P = .01		

SOURCE: Donnell M. Pappenfort, Clifton Rhodes, and Margaret Sebastian, "Factors Accounting for Variation in Use of Public Institutions for Delinquent Children in the United States and in Expenditures for Their Care," A Report of Research carried out under contract with the National Assessment Study of Correctional Programs for Juvenile and Youthful Offenders with support of Grant N172-014-6 to the University of Michigan by the United States Department of Justice, Law Enforcement Assistance Administration.

term (422 days) facility (B) had an average population of 147. The short-term (221 days) institution showed an average population of 249.

Pappenfort also found that long stay was associated with staff resources: "Private institutions for delinquent children in general have greater resources than do the public facilities and they tend to retain their charges for more extended periods of time".[16] Therefore we may assume that *a policy decision to expand the residential treatment model by hiring additional professional "treatment" personnel and constructing small institutions may only result in longer institution stay of youth assigned to these facilities.* It also suggests that, because of society's lower investment of "rehabilitation" resources in blacks, this group may experience more lenient sentences (days of incarceration) than whites assigned to these "treatment" facilities. But, the reverse may be true for *blacks assigned to traditional short-term "custody" settings.* Here, blacks *may expect a more severe sentence* compared to their white counterparts. These and additional social-policy considerations will be discussed in detail in the next chapter.

4
REFLECTIONS ON THE REVOLVING DOOR AND INSTITUTIONAL INDIVIDUALIZATION*

This chapter will demonstrate the degree to which the universally applied indeterminate sentence for the juvenile offender has been compromised by the necessities of the revolving door. That the latter is the social consequence of the former is also confirmed in this report.

Revolving Door Refined

There are three modes of entry or types of population input in public correctional institutions: new admissions, returnees, and interinstitutional transfers. There are two basic types of release: those youth that are transferred to another institution and the program-determined release in which a

---

*Originally appeared in Gerald R. Wheeler and D. Keith Nichols, "A Statistical Inquiry into Length of Stay and the Revolving Door: The Case for a Modified Fixed Sentence for the Juvenile Offender," *Monograph*, Ohio Youth Commission, April 1974.

youth is returned to the community. This report is concerned with the latter because most releases fall into this category.

The "revolving door" is defined as that situation in which a given state's institutions routinely admit new and repeating offenders but release them within a similar and predictable time frame extraneous to offender characteristics. To demonstrate the presence of the "revolving door" *between states*, we need to show that greater similarity than difference exists in states' average institutional stay controlling on offender and organizational variables. This was illustrated in Chapter 1 in which little difference on stay was observed when controlling on institution (population) size, use of parole board, classification systems, and offender characteristics.

To assert a "revolving-door" effect *in an institution within a state*, controlling on offender characteristics, we need to show that the "pattern of release" within a state's institution system is similar (regardless of offender characteristics). This is achieved by measuring the "speed" or the "revolutions" of the "revolving door" and stay, within each institution controlling on offender characteristics. To do this, we calculate the variation of residents' lengths of stay by a given characteristic, i.e., offense, from the total institution's average stay on that characteristic. The lower the variation found in the release pattern, the less individualization exhibited in the institution's release procedure and the faster the "revolutions" of the "revolving door." That is, although the total average length of stay may vary between institutions, given similar release patterns or velocity of revolutions, there will be minimal difference in the predictability of release or processing within the institution or within a category of offender. The thrust of the revolving-door argument lies in demonstrating a similar independent "institutional effect" on length of stay, regardless of offender characteristics. Each institution and offense category will exhibit the same "process" or release pattern indicative of low individualization and the "revolving door." Although institutions may appear on different points of the length-of-stay axis, this point is seen as arbitrary, reflecting the "time orientation" of that particular institution.

To better understand the above we will present the theoretical model applied to calculate the revolutions or velocity of the "revolving door" or degree of individualization among nine boy juvenile institutions.

Theoretical Assumptions

One of the goals of present-day juvenile corrections is that of "individualized treatment" of children committed to the system. "Individualized treatment" necessarily presupposes that each child will be treated according to his needs and not according to some abstract, predetermined, or generalized term of institutionalization.

This is in contrast to a system of warehousing children, which might best be described as institutions regulated by the "revolving door." This is a situation in which institutional stay is determined more by the "time orientation" and related population pressures of the institution than the individual offender. Inherent in this concept is that there is little difference in the lengths of stay of youth placed in the same institution.

A third type of system might be present, which could be called "generalized individual treatment." This would be where a general classification is used such as I-Level or commitment offense and each child categorized by that group's characteristics would be treated more or less in a similar manner. Most likely in this situation, each institution would have a specific treatment function and thus could be identified by a certain type of youth present.

To determine what type of system is being used in a correctional system, we can look at the curves of various characteristic variables measured against length of stay and graphically present whether certain conditions necessary for "individualized treatment" or the "revolving door" are present.

If "individualized treatment" is being used we would expect that the curve of the length of institutional stay would be relatively flat (see Figure 1). That is to say, if each youth is treated individually, there should be little relationship between the length of his institutional stay with that of any other youth. On the other hand, if we are merely "warehousing"

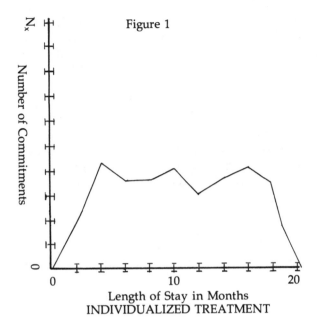

Figure 1

Length of Stay in Months
INDIVIDUALIZED TREATMENT

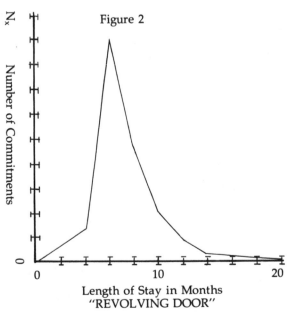

Figure 2

Length of Stay in Months
"REVOLVING DOOR"

50

children (the "revolving door"), we would expect a highly peaked curve (see Figure 2).

We can posit that as the width along the length-of-stay axis becomes narrower and the more peaked the curve becomes, that more children are getting out at a specific time. That is to say, the narrower the parameters and the higher the peak, the faster the "door" is revolving (see Figure 3).

Figure 3

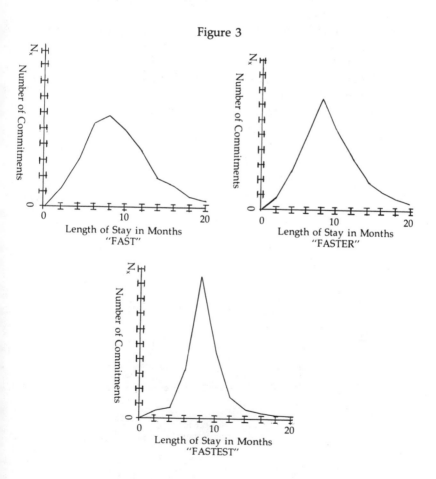

Given a highly peaked curve for length of stay, we can expect that for any variable compared with length of stay we would obtain a peaked curve. This phenomenon occurs because a highly peaked curve for the total population established relatively narrow parameters. The curves of any other variable with length of stay cannot fall outside of these parameters; therefore, it is not possible to have a variable with flat length-of-stay curves given a highly peaked total length-of-stay curve. Nor could we have a series of highly peaked curves, but at different points on the length-of-stay axis since some of these would inevitably have to fall outside the narrow parameters established by the length-of-stay curve for the total population (see Figure 4). In essence, if a "warehousing" effect is indicated by the length-of-stay curve for the total population, then it will be nearly the same for any variable.

On the other hand, a flat length-of-stay curve has several variations in interpretation that have to be taken into account.

Figure 4

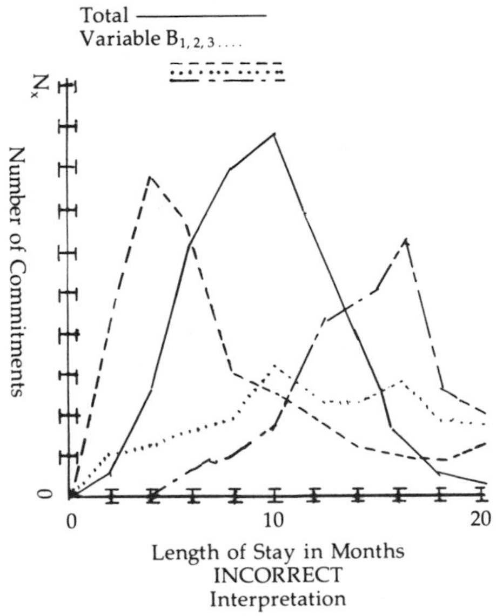

Total ——————
Variable $B_{1,2,3....}$

N_x
Number of Commitments

0   10   20

Length of Stay in Months
INCORRECT
Interpretation

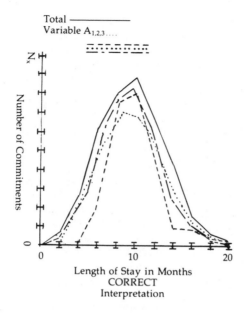

Total ———————
Variable $A_{1,2,3....}$

Number of Commitments

N_x

0

0   10   20

Length of Stay in Months
CORRECT
Interpretation

In the ideal "individualized treatment" situation (each child given specialized treatment), not only should the curve for length of stay of the total group be relatively flat, but the curve for any component variable should nearly mirror the curve for the total group (see Figure 5). This is because, in the ideal situation, there should be no group characteristic by which youth are classified (that would yield a series of more peaked curves).

Another situation that would cause a flat curve would be in the "generalized individual treatment" case. If a system such as I-Level or committing offense were used to classify children, we would expect a series of peaked curves for the individual variables, but whose location of the length-of-stay axis would be different. In other words, we would expect to find that in the I-Level case all I_3 CFM will be treated similarly, I_3 CFC similarly, etc. However, we should see significant variations in length of stay between any two component variables (see Figure 6).

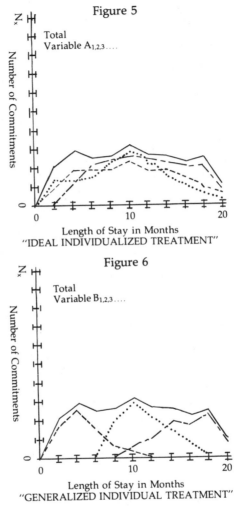

Figure 5

N_x

Number of Commitments

Total
Variable $A_{1,2,3}$....

0

0   10   20

Length of Stay in Months
"IDEAL INDIVIDUALIZED TREATMENT"

Figure 6

N_x

Number of Commitments

Total
Variable $B_{1,2,3}$....

0

0   10   20

Length of Stay in Months
"GENERALIZED INDIVIDUAL TREATMENT"

This situation could also be caused by each institution having a specific treatment function that would yield a peaked
curve for each institution, but a flatter curve for the total population. However, for these conditions to be met, any characteristic for the youth in that specific institution should be
relatively peaked or homogeneous. If the characteristics are

not homogeneous, then we can infer that instead of the type of youth determining the length of stay, there must be institutional factors at work determining how long a child stays.

A note to be added is that if we control for institutional size by using percentages in each length-of-stay category, instead of number of youth, then the curves may fall outside the curve of the total population and some variation in curves for each variable (such as institution) could be of different shape. The main argument for using this method is that if a large proportion of the population falls into one category of a variable, then what one is really measuring to a degree is the effect that that variable is having. For example, because 40 percent of State X's total male population goes to one institution (training school A), then by using total number of children, we are to a great extent measuring the effect that institution A is having on the population. On the other hand, by using percentages, we are giving equal weight to each institution.

In summary, we are able to test whether "individualized treatment" is being used by the curve of the length of stay. A flat curve must be present if the conditions for "individualized treatment" are met. A peaked curve shows that we are warehousing children. This theoretical model will be used to investigate what is happening within nine State X institutions.

Length of Stay and Individualized Treatment: The Case of State X

Using the theoretical model previously discussed, we will proceed to investigate the application of "individualized treatment" on 528 males permanently committed to State X's Youth Commission in April, May, and June 1972. Percentages of commitments are used in developing the graphs so that each component of the variables plotted will have equal weight.

When the length of stay for the total population is graphed, we obtain a highly peaked curve that tails off toward the longer stay end (see Figure 7). The inference here is that although we may later find particular components of selected variables showing inclinations toward "individualized treatment," the general situation is characterized by the "revolving door." In fact, 70% of the population has lengths of stay between 5½ to 8 months. That is to say, seven out of every ten youths stay in an institution for a period of time differing no more than ten weeks.

Figure 7

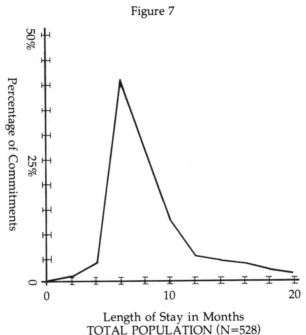

Length of Stay in Months
TOTAL POPULATION (N=528)

While there are major differences in the average lengths of stay (see Table 1), we observe that the "revolving door" is present within the institutions. All of the institutions with the exception of C, H, and F have highly peaked curves within relatively narrow parameters characteristic of the "revolving door." Even in the three exceptions, the pattern is found. However, at C and H facilities this effect is somewhat muted because more than half of the commitments remained longer than the original peak.

This situation would seem to indicate that a "generalized individual treatment" method was in operation within State

X's institutions. However, for this to be correct, we must show that there are certain identifiable common characteristics present and that these youth are sent to particular institutions. At the time this group of children were committed, I-Level was not being used, so we can discard it as a classification system. We found no statistical significance between commitment of-

Figure 8

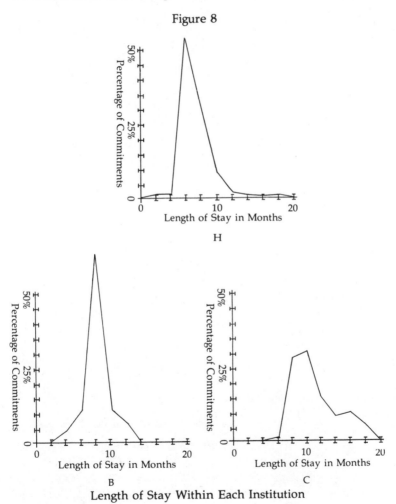

Length of Stay Within Each Institution

Figure 8 (cont.)

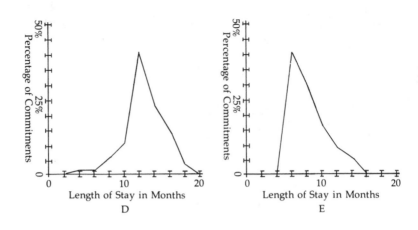

D

E

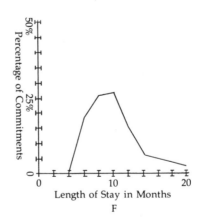

F

Figure 8 (cont.)

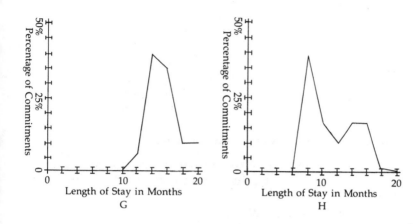

G

H

I

Table 1

RELATIONSHIP BETWEEN INSTITUTIONS AND
AVERAGE LENGTH OF STAY[a]—NINE MALE INSTITUTIONS

Institution	Average Stay in Months
A	7.0
B	7.4
C	10.6
D	10.2
E	7.8
F	9.4
G	16.3
H	10.3
I	14.0

[a]Includes diagnostic placement (average 6 week); 487 cases

fenses and the institution to which a youth was sent, although
there was a trend in that institution H received less serious offenders.

When the lengths of stay for the four major categories of
offense were graphed for the total sample population, we find
nearly the same curve for each group (see Figure 9).

Figure 9

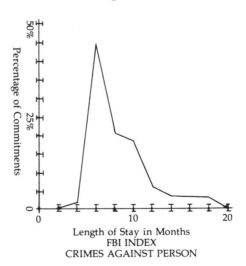

Length of Stay in Months
FBI INDEX
CRIMES AGAINST PERSON

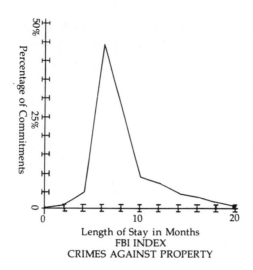

Percentage of Commitments

Length of Stay in Months
FBI INDEX
CRIMES AGAINST PROPERTY

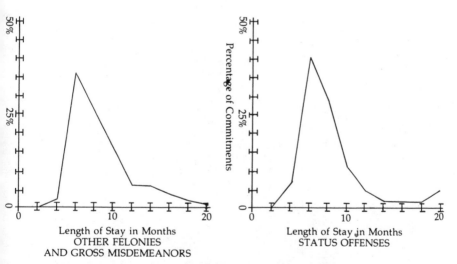

Percentage of Commitments

Length of Stay in Months
OTHER FELONIES
AND GROSS MISDEMEANORS

Percentage of Commitments

Length of Stay in Months
STATUS OFFENSES

The importance of this finding is that not only do we not keep a serious offender significantly longer than a status offender (equal parameters), but that the rate of "revolutions" of the "revolving door" are nearly equal.

With race, we found that although whites had a tendency

to stay slightly longer (less than a month), the curves are nearly identical (see Figure 10). The only difference is that the curve for nonwhites shows a slightly faster "revolving-door" effect.

Figure 10

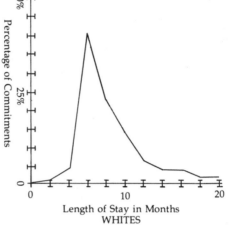

Length of Stay in Months
WHITES

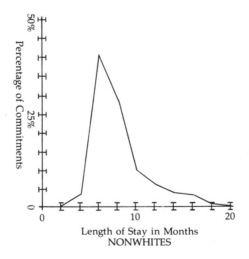

Length of Stay in Months
NONWHITES

The first salient finding relating to offender characteristics was that age was found associated with institution assignment ($X^2 = 274.8$, P = .001) and institutional length of stay (see Table 2) when controlling on institutions. Figure 11 shows the curves of the length of stay for each age group. The 10 to 14 age group shows the first difference in any of the curves that we have so far looked at.

The "revolving door" is spinning at a rapid pace for the three older age groups. In fact, Table 6 shows, of the four institutions with a 10 to 14 age group, these youngsters stayed longer in three facilities and the same as the 15-year-olds in one setting. In only one institution (I) were the 15-year-olds released sooner (one month) than the older youth.

Since we could find no formal system being used to place different types of children in particular institutions and there was no significant relationship between length of stay and any particular variable except for the youngest age group, we could but conclude that *institutions were invariably discriminating against the youngest offender in terms of period of confinement*. It will be argued that this proves that "treatment" objectives are central for youngest groups. Discriminating against the youngest in releasing criteria and duration of incarceration is seen as

Table 2

RELATIONSHIP BETWEEN INSTITUTIONAL STAY AND AGE BY INSTITUTION[a]—NINE MALE INSTITUTIONS

INSTITUTION	YEARS OF AGE			
	10-14	15	16	17 and over
A	6.7(Mos.)	6.7	6.3	6.5
B		7.2	7.0	6.6
C	11.6	9.0	8.0	8.5
D	9.6	8.8		
E			8.2	6.6
F		9.3	8.7	10.8
G	16.5	14.5	15.5	
H	9.8			
I			14.0	13.3
Total Average	10.8	9.3	9.7	8.7

[a]Includes diagnostic placement (average 6 weeks); 487 cases

Figure 11

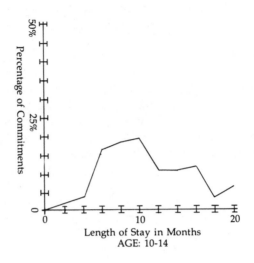

Length of Stay in Months
AGE: 10-14

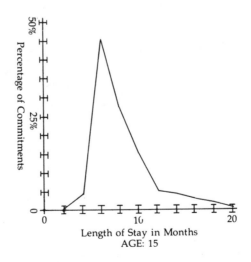

Length of Stay in Months
AGE: 15

64

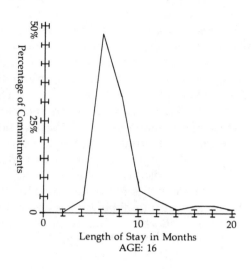

Length of Stay in Months
AGE: 16

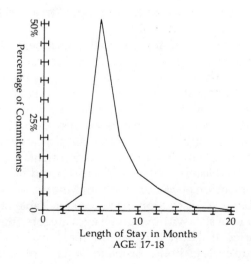

Length of Stay in Months
AGE: 17-18

65

appropriately applying correctional resources during a youth's "impressionable years" and thus deters further acts of delinquency. This argument flies in the face of the findings on the effects of "prisonization" on the youngest age group.

This analysis found that for major (index) offenders ages 10 through 14, return status or recidivism was associated with longer institution length of stay. For minor (nonindex) offenders, success on parole was associated with slightly longer institution stay. But, because many in this category include status offenders, it would be expected that age alone would bias the success rate. (The longer a status is incarcerated the less likely that he will be returned—for a status offense.) The relationship between "prisonization" and parole success for this group (status offenders) is not determined by "treatment" experienced in the institution, but by age alone. In regard to the youngest group with serious offenses at time of commitment, this investigation indicated that *longer length of stay in institutions and more "treatment," as reflected in the releasing criteria, increased the chances of returning to unlawful acts.* These results hardly suggest that there is a significant payoff in reducing crime and delinquency by deliberately subjecting youngest offenders to longer sentences and more "treatment"—regardless of crime at commitment.

To assure that institutional adjustment was not influencing length of stay for certain age groups, this relationship was tested. Using indicators designed to measure adjustment in State X's diagnostic center, where youth spend approximately six weeks before institutional assignment, no statistical difference was found between age groups. Because there was no relationship between the youth's diagnostic center adjustment and "permanent" institutional assignment, we assumed that "poorer" adjusters were equally distributed in all the facilities. Neither can we posit a unique community "home" problem on the youngest institutionalized group; Table 2 shows more variation of stay within a given age category than between age categories. If duration of confinement was a function of the community, e.g. home problem or lack of resources, in the youngest age group, we will expect a more uniform release pattern for this group between institutions. The opposite pattern was observed. The same conclusion applies to the argument that special education programs, e.g. vocational, academic, determine stay. If age is highly tied to these programs, we would expect minimal variation on this factor among institutions.

These findings strengthen our conclusion that, *next to institutional assignment, age itself, was the most important factor determining institutional length of stay.* In view of the above, to what do we attribute younger boys' length of stay in State X's institutions?

The Child Welfare Effect

The investigators concluded that each institution operated its own revolving door, regulating the speed of the revolutions to unwittingly deselect the more undesirable or socially unattractive resident. Conversely, the revolutions assured keeping the younger and often least serious offender longer to facilitate "treatment." The "child welfare effect" was seen in the greater exercise of staff discretion in releasing the young offender. Release of the older and often hard-core delinquent appeared more automatic and sooner. That age appeared as the most significant client characteristic related to institutional stay is interpreted as an unanticipated consequence of the juvenile courts' philosophy of *parens patria* and related indeterminate sentence, married and reinforced by social work's historical and fervent commitment to providing "treatment" programs. The magnitude of this orientation was apparent in the findings on other states in which few agencies associated the offender with offense. At the same time we found that, nationally, state release patterns vary only slightly.

State correctional agencies do not have the luxury of controlled intake. This coupled with the indeterminate sentence leads to inevitable institutional overload. To release the pressure, a valve or regulator is necessary. The revolving door constitutes the valve. In this respect, the nation and state each have a network of revolving doors that are activated according to political climate and social condition. To accommodate a public outcry against street crime, either more institutions are constructed or the length of institutional stay is reduced. Paradoxically, not the least serious negative social consequence of the latter is reducing the length of stay of the very offender whom society fears the most. Whereas, if new facilities are built, given the indeterminate sentence, the youngest, and for the most part, the youth least associated with street crime and violent acts, will stay longer.

Therefore, we submit that there is no evidence that the clinical or protective social-control assumptions of juvenile justice have been met. This applies to states that have adopted classification treatment systems or continue to employ traditional intuitive methods of assignment and "treatment." Indeed, "time is a waste of time." The older and perhaps most dangerous offender will not perceive time as a deterrent to crime because he gets out earlier. Whereas, the young and more likely less serious offender remains in the institution for supposedly "socialization"—a child welfare function—which can better be accomplished in the community. But even for this group, little "individualization" is demonstrated in that ultimately they merely stay longer. More money won't help!

Money and Revolutions

No amount of money or increase in "credentialed" staff will counter the abuses of a correctional system governed by the indeterminate sentence and its resultant irrational revolving-door system. Since 1970, there has been approximately a 16 percent decrease of population in state juvenile facilities. But during this period there was also an increase of local community detention facilities.[1] This is a function of the various state subsidy programs that offer locals financial incentive to construct smaller and more "humane" institutions. This may raise the standards of the institutional practice, but it does not reduce the number of incarcerated youth. It merely distributes the revolving-door paradox locally, and perhaps effects a delayed entry into the state system.

Given the paradox of the "revolving door" and related "child welfare effect," we may anticipate that alleged "individual treatment" or rehabilitation under the ruse of "proven" or "experimental" behavior-modification techniques, will be enthusiastically applied in heavier and more expensive doses to effect institutional adjustment on the youth mostly suffering from family and school problems and the least serious offenders. Older, and already "institutionalized" youthful felons will continue to "beat the clock."

Voluntary private agencies will not help. As apparent as the "child welfare effect" is in the public correctional system, it appears even more so in the private sector. Residential "treatment" institutions continue their long-standing practice of selecting the most socially attractive "low-risk" problem youngster. While most of these agencies receive public funding, there is no mechanism to prevent or control discriminatory admission practices. Private institutions regulate intake to assure long length of stay of residents, which in turn facilitates a "stable institutional culture" and a reasonable number of "success" cases. Such policies and practices provide evidence and justification for continued fiscal support from the community and the board of directors.

So entrenched is the "child welfare effect" in the private sector that it often literally discounts the problem of youthful crime and delinquency. This development is vividly illustrated in a 1972 newspaper investigation of Boys Town's operations.[2] Most of the child welfare and delinquency experts contacted by the reporters "regarded Boys Town's large single-institution approach as inadequate for the kinds of problems children face today."[3] In 1972, the administration was characterized as "tight budgeted," "conservative," and authoritarian in treatment of its residents.[4] All boys' incoming mail was read, meals were held in a giant mess hall, and residents' use of telephones was forbidden.[5]

But the focus of the investigation was not centered on the "treatment" of boys but on the funding operation of Boys Town. Upon examining public documents it was discovered that comparing Boys Town's wealth ($191.5 million) in 1970 to that of other institutions (Boys Town's endowment was about three times Notre Dame's; its net worth would have ranked it 230th on *Fortune's* list of the 'top 500' industrial firms).[6]

It was estimated that Boys Town also received $200,000 annually in public funds. Most significant, its elaborate soliciting program was bringing in $15 million each year—twice the cost of operating the institution. By 1973, Boys Town's net worth jumped to $226.7 million.[7]

As a result of the newspaper exposé in 1972, Boys Town reduced its population to near 500, dropped the practice of censoring mail, and gave residents' telephone privileges in the pay phones in the cottages. In terms of program, the reaction to negative publicity was to start work on $10.1 million building for the Boys Town Institute for Communication Disorders in Children. Also construction was planned on the Center for the Study of Youth Development, with facilities in Omaha, Washington, D.C., and Palo Alto, California. "Because of the threat of lawsuits charging misuse of funds that earlier donors gave for orphanage programs, Boys Town is funding the project through new funding letters."[8] The above event is representative of contemporary "successful" private child-welfare programs, a program that in the days of Father Flanagan concentrated on helping delinquent and homeless youth. Now with a surplus budget, the Boys Town administration—influenced by the "child-welfare effect"—is investing *not* in community-based rehabilitation programs aimed at "delinquent" and wayward youth, but in children's communication disorders and research! We may, from these developments, surmise that delinquency has been conquered. Sadly, what it really means, is that working with the classic delinquent is not conducive to fund-raising and organizational expansion.

If the "child-welfare effect" is exhibited in the institutional phase of the correctional process, what is its relationship to parole supervision? This and other questions on juvenile parole will be explored in Chapter 5.

5
JUVENILE PAROLE: EXTENDING THE THERAPEUTIC STATE

Introduction

In the middle nineteenth century, Captain Alexander Maconochie proposed to the House of Commons a "scheme of marks awarded for industry, labor and good conduct."[1] Referred to as a "ticket-of-leave" license, his program gave prisoners an opportunity to earn their way out of confinement. Today, Maconochie's concept is universal in American adult corrections.[2] In juvenile corrections, 70 percent of delinquents are now released from institutions under a parole or aftercare program.[3] In 1974, 25 percent of the states reported operating a bona fide parole board.[4] In view of the growing criticism of adult parole, it seems appropriate to evaluate its application on juveniles.

Focus of Study

The purpose of the study is to test major assumptions[5] of parole or aftercare as they pertain to the juvenile justice system. It will attempt to ascertain a) the effect of parole on sentencing, b) the degree to which the contract between the recipient of parole and granting authority is complied with, and c) the nature and extent of supervision in the community.

To assess the effect of parole on juvenile sentencing, we analyzed the parole practices of a large Midwestern state. Technically, State X does not have a juvenile parole board. However, a release recommendation from its community aftercare branch, with final approval of the central administration classification section, must be obtained before a youth leaves an institution. Upon release, a youth will be supervised by a "youth counselor" whom he refers to as his "P.O." (parole officer). In the community, he is subject to the conditions of parole for a period not to exceed his twenty-first birthday. In regard to parole revocation, the "P.O." has the authority to return a violator to an institution without a court hearing. Thus, on an operational level, this state has implemented a juvenile parole program.

Parole and Sentencing

If an explicit parole policy was formulized statewide, we would expect some evidence of uniformity in sentencing controlling on individual factors such as age, race, or offense. Such was not the case. Depending on the institution, sentences for male offenders committed on crimes against the person ranged from 191 to 562 average days; stay for 15-year-olds showed a low of 197 days and high of 726 days. In addition, we would expect some manifestation of concern by the central administration in regard to releasing serious offenders. However, the reverse was apparent. In half of the institutions, the least-serious-offenders category was associated with longest stay. Therefore, these results seem to indicate that the parole mechanism was triggered by the institution and that sentencing was not significantly affected by the presence of a parolelike operation.

These findings contrast parole studies on adults, which consistently show that parole boards are sensitive to severity

of offense.[6] This may be attributed to minimum sentencing policies, which link confinement to the gravity of crime. Parole
boards also tend to increase the length of stay of adult offenders.[7]

To determine the degree to which youth succeed on
parole, an analysis of State X's parole outcome by region was
conducted.

Parole Revocation

Between January 1 and June 30, 1974, State X's institutions
released 1,116 youth to the community. During this period 357
or 32 percent were returned by the youth counselor or recommitted (readjudicated) to institutions. Table 1 offers a regional
breakdown of parole outcome.

Table 1

PAROLE OUTCOME BY PERCENT AND AVERAGE TIME
UNDER SUPERVISION—SIX MONTHS—1974

Region	Re-leased	Re-turned/ Recom-mitted	Time on Parole Before R/R	Percent R/R	Average Regional Community Supervision
A	156	63	7.8 (months)	40%	11.0 (months)
B*	74	31	5.6	41	8.8
C	152	55	7.0	36	12.7
D	259	61	9.9	23	13.0
E	191	66	6.8	35	8.3
F	137	48	7.7	35	10.4
G	147	33	6.7	23	10.5
	——	——	7.8	32	11.2
State total	1116	357			

*Rural

Limited control precluded comparing the outcomes of parole
and nonparole supervised groups. We were able to examine
the relationship of length of parole to revocation in similar-
size parole regions.

Considerable difference was observed in average parole

time and percent of revocation between the two largest urban parole districts (D and E). Region E not only had a shorter parole and higher return rate, it revoked parole sooner. The region (D) that showed the higher average length of parole for total offenders (13.0 months) was associated with the lower (23 percent) return rate. Also alike in population and location, regions F and G showed similar disparity in return rate but not in average time of parole. To better ascertain whether regional parole practices influence return rate, we calculated return rate for the three "longest" and "shortest" parole regions. Regions A, C, and D averaged 12.3 months in community supervision and showed a return rate of 36.5. This compared to 37.0 percent return for regions B, E, and F, which only supervised parolees for slightly over nine months. Even if we compare time on parole at time of revocation, there was no difference in return rate. The three regions that imposed parole revocation the soonest (6.3 months) showed nearly the same return rate (33 percent) as the three regions that delayed (8.4 months) revocation (32.7 percent).

These results seem to suggest that neither length of parole at revocation or for the regional group as a whole affect return rate. If revocation was a function of formal policy we would expect an increase in parole time to produce a higher return rate, as the period of vulnerability is extended. Conversely, a shorter parole period would reduce the rate of return. An alternative explanation is that time will not affect return rate because revocation is a function of individual regions' unique interpretation of parole regulations. Under one set of conditions, a youth will not be returned until he violates a rule. In the other, he may break a rule and not be returned because of a region's lenient parole standards. In this study, the results point to the latter in that comparable regions that exhibited the same time frame in overall parole supervision show different return rates; and regions that exhibited the same return rates were found to have varying lengths of parole for both returners and the parolee population as a whole. A "regional effect" is also evident when we compare the largest and black-dominated urban parole district with the smallest and white-dominated rural district. Region B (rural), which tended to return violators the soonest (5.6 months), had the highest return rate (41 percent). In contrast, region D (urban), which waited the longest (9.9 months), showed the lowest rate (23 percent) of return.

Therefore, it appears that duration of parole as well as the criteria of revocation is more a function of the individual region than the characteristics of the offender or the community. Thus, it is evident that much of the activity of parole officers consists of arbitrarily recycling youth through the institutions. The negative consequences of imposing parole without a central policy or standard will become more apparent in the next paragraph.

Parole Distribution

The third assumption of parole is the provision of supervision under ordinary social conditions. This question will be answered by determining the levels of parole or "who" gets "how much" supervision. Table 2 shows the distribution of parole in average days of State X's 1972 three month cohort by sex, race, and offense. These data include only cases that were not returned or recommitted to an institution. Length of parole

Table 2

AVERAGE LENGTH OF PAROLE BY OFFENSE,
SEX, AND RACE OF 1972 COHORT—501 CASES

Offense	Female		Male	
	White	Black	White	Black
Type I (FBI Index Against Person)	278[a]	238	202	342
Type II (FBI Index Against Property)	290	234	202	305
Type III (Other Felonies and Misd.)	336	334	275	328
Type IV (Juvenile Status and Misd.)	301	326	307	352
Total Average	331	324	292	325

[a]Days

is defined as average days a youth is supervised in the community from institutional release to parole discharge or to the end of the study.

While not statistically significant, this data showed a consistent pattern of racial discrimination in parole practices among males regardless of offense at commitment. Blacks averaged over a month longer parole than whites in three of four offense categories. Black status offenders averaged nearly two months longer (352 days) than white Type I index offenders (302 days). The shortest length of parole (275 days) appeared in the white Type III category. The longest (352 days) period of supervision was associated with black status or Type IV group. This pattern was somewhat reversed among females. Whites had longer parole in three of four offense categories. However, in the status offender group—69 percent of the total female parole cases—blacks showed longer parole. We also observed that black female status offenders experienced longer parole supervision than white index offenders.

Comparing sex and parole duration, the findings indicated that females are subject to slightly longer community supervision than males. This result is mostly accounted for by white Type III offenders who average 50 days longer parole than their male counterparts.

The Age Factor

To determine the effect of age on length of parole, this variable was held constant. Table 3 shows the average length of parole of 385 males. As expected, "short" parole was associated with the oldest age group (17 years and older). It may be asserted that a lower mean parole score for this group is explained by these youth reaching the mandatory discharge age (21 years). But our analysis of institutional stay showed that older offenders experienced more lenient sentences and indeed were eligible for parole for 1000 or more days. In other words, "short" parole for older offenders was an informal policy effect, undoubtably influenced by State X's disinclination to return older parole violators to a "juvenile" facility. A one-way analysis of variance shows that difference on age and parole duration could be attributed to chance less than one out of 100 times (F=7.88—females; F=22.28 males).[8]

Table 3

AVERAGE LENGTH OF PAROLE OF MALES
BY RACE, AGE, AND OFFENSE—385 CASES

Offense	Age							
	10-14 yrs		15 yrs		16 yrs		17 and over	
	White	Black	White	Black	White	Black	White	Black
Type I	560[a]	393	480	388	303	374	187	253
Type II	304	318	356	333	324	367	223	238
Type III	274	436	350	412	340	378	206	236
Type IV	427	371	284	363	222	319	272	-a

[a]Days

If parole is perceived as a "punitive" sanction, the above results demonstrate the lack of equal punishment. We may question the justice of subjecting the youngest offender (10 to 14 years) from twice to four times longer parole supervision than the oldest group (17 years and over) given similar offense history. For example, what is the social value of policing one youngster in the community committed to a correctional agency on a major index crime six months and another 18 months? If parole is seen as a "rehabilitation" function, the emphasis would seem to be on helping youth remain in the community and avoid incarceration. However, this is contradicted in the over-representation of young offenders returned on parole violation (see Table 4).

Table 4

PERCENT OF MALE YOUTH RETURNED WITHIN EACH AGE
CATEGORY BY RACE—503 CASES

Race	Age			
	10-14 years	15 yrs	16 yrs	17 and over
Black	33 (percent)	37	20	7
White	47	36	30	9

Moreover, most parole violations fall in the "technical, no-new-offense" category.* In view of the marked pattern of extending parole for the youngest offender category (this was true in all categories except 10-14 years white Type I and II and black Type II), it may be concluded that State X's parole practice is significantly determined by age. Table 3 also confirms the importance of race in determining parole. Controlling on age and offense at commitment, blacks averaged longer parole in 11 of 16 possible categories. The highest variations (162 days) was found in the 10-14-year-old Type III offense category.

Among females, age and race discrimination was less apparent. The shortest parole (207 days) was observed in the white Type II 15-year-old category. The longest parole (400 days) appeared in Type III group in this age and race category. "Long" parole was generally associated with younger offenders. But this was mostly evident in the nonindex (Type III, IV) offense categories. Ten-to-fourteen-year-old black Type III offenders averaged 104 more days of parole than their 17-year-old-and-older counterparts. The youngest white status group had 146 average days longer on parole than the oldest category.

Offense at Commitment

In contrast to males, where offense appeared a weak predictor of parole, among females there was a consistent pattern of extended parole for the less serious offense categories (Type III, IV). White 15-year-old property offenders averaged 207 days of community supervision. This compares to 400 and 352 average days for nonindex and status offenders. The same was true for blacks. Sixteen-year-old Type I offenders showed 244

---

*The significance of discretionary authority is measured in the following statistics. In 1973, 562 (73 percent) of State X's 776 parole revocations were returned to institutions on the recommendation of the parole officer without a court hearing. Three hundred fifty-one of these youth (62 percent) were returned on a "technical" parole violation (no new offenses or juvenile status offenses). This compared to 38 percent in this category recommitted to institutions by the court. Thus we observe that the vast majority of youth are reinstitutionalized on technical violations initiated by parole officers.

days "less" parole time than their status counterparts. Thus for females, parole is more reserved for the least serious and younger law violator.

Alternative Assumptions

One may speculate that "long" parole for blacks is explained by "prior" offenses or shorter length of institution stay and not race. The first assumption discounts the results of most research. "The single most important finding" of Wolfgang's et al. monumental study, *Delinquency in a Birth Cohort* "was that nonwhite youth consistently got more severe dispositions. This difference held up . . . irrespective of difference in prior record, and whether the offense was 'index' or 'nonindex'."[9] In regard to sentencing, there was a trend of "reverse" discrimination among males and females in long-term "treatment" institutions. But in those categories in which blacks (males) showed significantly "longer" confinement than whites (2 months—Type IV) blacks still show longer parole. Among females, blacks who show "longer" length institutional stays (Type III and IV), also evidenced longer or equivalent parole supervision.

That extended parole characterizes the experience of the majority of black cases regardless of offense suggests that parole may be perceived by agency personnel and society as more punitive than rehabilitative. But, considering the fact that younger offenders were inclined to receive longer parole irrespective of race or offense at commitment, it may well be that community supervision is seen as more "paternalistic" or rehabilitative than "protective." Also, while sexism is apparent in the intake phase (majority of female commitments fall in the status category), the findings on institutional stay and parole go against the notion that females experience more or less "treatment" or "punishment" postcommitments because of their sex. As a group, females suffer no less abuses inherent in the indeterminate sentence and parole than males.

To a significant degree, length-of-parole findings reflect the same pattern of age discrimination observed in institutional stay. Also, notwithstanding parole disparities between specific categories, and a regional effect, the overall pattern of community supervision suggests considerable uniformity in State X's parole practices. We ponder the desirability of uniform parole time for different classes of offenders. Under this scheme, the "risk" or danger to the community is ignored. To the offender, who may see parole as punishment, uniform parole time is inherently inequitable, unless, of course, it is limited to the gravity of the crime or illegal act.

Social Consequences of Parole Inequities

Parole inequities contribute to neither social control nor rehabilitation. In terms of fulfilling its social-control function, it is difficult to defend a discretion-oriented parole policy that results in providing equal or longer community supervision for status offenders (runaways, incorrigibles) than youth committed on serious FBI index crimes. This, in effect, depletes scarce manpower resources that could better be utilized to supervise "high-risk" offenders in the community. Assigning status offenders parole officers also prejudices these youth's standing with teachers, employers, and the community who will likely associate them with felons. Thirdly, there is little justification for unequal policing of similar law violators unless the agency can demonstrate its functions as a special deterrent to crime. Heretofore, no evidence to this effect has been presented. In this instance, a juvenile correctional agency's penchant for indeterminate parole can only be matched by its undaunted loyalty to the indeterminate sentence.

Conclusion: Extension of Therapeutic State

These findings raise serious doubts as to the ability of parole to fulfill its historical mission. There was no evidence to support the premise that parole significantly affects sentences or recidivism. The return rate of regions ranged from a low 23 to a high 41 percent. But the analysis showed no relationship between duration of parole supervision and return. Of the three assumptions of parole, the nature of supervision in the

community most dramatically illustrates the negative consequences of the indeterminate parole. Regardless of offense,
blacks generally received longer parole than whites. The same
trend of longer parole was observed for younger offenders and
females. Also, youth with the least serious offense at commitment were subject to equal or longer supervision in the community than index offenders. *In conclusion, these findings show
the degree to which parole functions are an extension of the therapeutic state. Like institution sentences, length of parole is determined
more by the personality of the region, the age and race of the offender,
than the needs of the individual or the community.* In the absence of
major changes in social policy, counteracting the "child-welfare effect" and other abuses of the indeterminate sentence will
depend on constructive measures taken by correctional administrators. This is the focus of the following chapter.

II

The Social-Policy Mission:
Issues and Answers on
Juvenile Justice Reform

6
ATTITUDES TOWARD
A FIXED SENTENCE
FOR JUVENILE OFFENDERS

These research findings present a strong case against continuing the indeterminate sentence. While many lawyers and criminologists agree with this conclusion, correctional practitioners appear highly sceptical of adopting a "fixed" sentence for juveniles. To assess the official attitude toward a fixed sentence linked to seriousness of offense, a summary of the author's study outlining the heretofore-described sentencing disparities, along with the survey instrument, was mailed to 286 state juvenile correctional superintendents listed in the 1972 American Correctional Association Directory.[1] While only 78, or 27 percent, of the superintendents contacted responded, they appeared representative of the nation as a whole. The sample included superintendents from 66 percent of the states in all nine United States census regions. Even within census regions, only two areas showed less than a majority of state participation. Attitude toward a "fixed" sentence was derived by using a 16-point scale. Table 1 shows the general characteristics of the institutions sampled.

The study was primarily concerned with examining the

Table 1

CHARACTERISTICS OF 78 JUVENILE INSTITUTIONS
SURVEYED IN 1974 BY PERCENT

Characteristic	Number	Percent
Classification System:		
I-Level & Quay	34	44%
APA & Other	44	56
Total	78	100%
Parole Board Status:		
Parole Board	29	37%
Nonparole Board	49	63
Total	78	100%
Year(s) Institution Built[a]:		
1866-1899	17	22%
1900-1924	17	22
1925-1948	4	5
1952-1972	38	50
Total	76	100%
Cost Per Child Per Day[b]:		
$11 & below	2	3%
$12-$20	21	34
$21-$30	21	34
$31 & over	17	28
Average Daily Population[c]:		
(male, female & co-ed		
institutions combined)		
50 & below	10	14%
51-150	36	49
151-300	17	23
301 & over	10	14
Total	73	100%

(percentage rounded)

[a]2 (3%) did not report year institution was built
[b]17 (22%) did not report cost per child per day
[c]5 (6%) did not report average daily population

attitude of superintendents in relationship to their institutions. The following section will attempt to show under what conditions or specific offenses will superintendents from a given type of institution endorse a "fixed" sentence.

Institution Population

Table 2 shows that superintendents from lower-populated institutions (99 or less residents) tend to endorse a "fixed" sentence for less serious offenses more than their high-population counterparts (100 or more residents). For example, 26 percent of the former endorse a "fixed" sentence for "breaking and entering." This compared to only eight percent of the high-populated institutions in this category. However, we observe minimal variation on attitude with regard to the more serious offenses. Also, the highest proportion, 42 percent, of endorsements was found in the category "homicide" in high-populated institutions.

Table 2

RELATIONSHIP BETWEEN SIZE OF INSTITUTION AND ATTITUDE TOWARD A MODIFIED FIXED SENTENCE BY PERCENT OF SUPERINTENDENTS ENDORSING A MODIFIED FIXED SENTENCE. N = 63 SUPERINTENDENTS[a]

Offense	Institutions With 99 & Under	Institutions With 100 & Over
Homicide	41%	42%
Armed Robbery	37	36
Aggravated Assault	26	25
Runaway	19	19
School Truancy	19	17
Breaking & Entering	26	8
Drugs for Sale	30	14
Auto Theft	26	8
	N = 27	N = 36

[a]15 did not respond to average daily population

Parole Boards

The method of release did not appear to influence the superintendents' attitude toward a "fixed" sentence. Table 3 shows that only a slightly higher proportion of superintendents governed by parole boards (64 percent) than nonparole boards (59 percent) endorsed a "fixed" sentence for "armed robbery." It is interesting to note that a higher percentage of superintendents endorsed a fixed sentence for "armed robbery" than "homicide."

Table 3

RELATIONSHIP BETWEEN METHOD OF RELEASE AND ATTITUDE TOWARD A MODIFIED FIXED SENTENCE BY PERCENT OF SUPERINTENDENTS ENDORSING A MODIFIED FIXED SENTENCE. N = 78 SUPERINTENDENTS

Offense	Parole Boards	Nonparole Boards
Homicide	44%	41%
Armed Robbery	64	59
Aggravated Assault	24	24
Runaway	16	17
School Truancy	16	17
Breaking & Entering	16	17
Drugs for Sale	20	21
Auto Theft	16	17
	N = 49	N = 29

Classification System

Table 4 suggests considerable variation on attitude between superintendents using the Interpersonal Maturity Scale (I-Level) and/or Quay and those employing the traditional American Psychological Association index (APA) and other classification systems. I-Level and Quay superintendents consistently showed a higher endorsement rating. Their percentage of endorsement for a "fixed" sentence ranged from a 50 percent high for "homicide" to a 17 percent low for status and minor offenses. Whereas, the range of the traditional classification group was from a high of 35 percent for "homicide" to a low of 15 percent for "school truancy," "breaking and entering," and "auto theft."

Table 4

RELATIONSHIP BETWEEN CLASSIFICATION SYSTEMS AND
ATTITUDE TOWARD A MODIFIED FIXED SENTENCE BY
PERCENT OF SUPERINTENDENTS ENDORSING A MODIFIED
FIXED SENTENCE. TOTAL N = 78 SUPERINTENDENTS

Offense	I-Level & Quay	APA & Other
Homicide	50%	35%
Armed Robbery	33	32
Aggravated Assault	28	22
Runaway	17	17
School Truancy	17	15
Breaking & Entering	17	15
Drugs for Sale	17	20
Auto Theft	17	15
	N = 18	N = 60

Institutional Cost, Length of Stay, and Receptivity to a Fixed Sentence

Because higher institution costs and longer stay are generally associated with private "treatment oriented" facilities,[2] it
was hypothesized that superintendents from this type of public institution will be less favorable toward a "fixed" sentence.
Using the median per diem cost, average length of stay, and
attitude score, Table 5 indicates that this hypothesis was only
partially supported. Superintendents of high-cost institutions
consistently showed a higher endorsement than their low-cost
counterparts. This was particularly true among those respondents associated with short-term, high-cost facilities. However, using a total group average, long-term institutions exhib-

Table 5

RELATIONSHIP BETWEEN INSTITUTION PER-DAY COST,
LENGTH OF STAY, AND PERCENT ENDORSING
A FIXED SENTENCE. 61 SUPERINTENDENTS

	Percent Endorsing Stay	
Per-Day Cost	0-7.0 months	7.1 months and over
$23 and under	40%	38%
$24 and over	54	41
Total Average	47	40

ited a less favorable response (40 percent) than facilities that released youth sooner (47 percent). These data support Pappenfort's conclusion that long-term public institutions, which so characterize private institutions for delinquent youth, will strongly oppose abolishing the indeterminate sentence.

We would expect superintendents who perceive institutionalization as punishment to opt for a shorter stay and perhaps a fixed sentence related to seriousness of the offense. This may explain the higher rate of endorsement when controlling on cost. But as the graph below suggests (see Table 6), a vast proportion of superintendents responded on the negative extreme of the continuum.

Table 6

DISTRIBUTION OF SUPERINTENDENTS'
ATTITUDE SCORE TOWARD A "FIXED" SENTENCE

Interval	f	Percent
0-2	45	58%
3-5	6	8
6-8	15	19
9-11	0	0
12-14	5	6
15 and over	7	9
Total	78	100%

Nearly 40 percent of the superintendents sampled flatly rejected the determinate sentence for the juvenile offender regardless of the offense. A third indicated a "moderate" endorsement, having a score of eight or above. A few scored 16, suggesting that they were unequivocally opposed to the indeterminate sentence.*

Summary of Statistical Findings

Table 7 illustrates the lack of statistical evidence supporting any notion that attitude toward a "fixed" sentence is a function of institution-related factors, as reflected in its super-

---

*The attitude score was determined by giving equal weight to each offense endorsed (+1 point) by superintendents, subtracting each negative response (−1 point), plus adding the constant 8. No answer was equivalent to zero.

intendent's attitude. Due to the skewed distribution of data, the chi-square statistic was employed. The highest chi-square score, .9119 (not significant), was observed when comparing the differences in attitude between old (built before 1950) and new institutions (built in 1950 and after). A greater proportion (10 percent variation) of superintendents administering old institutions scored 4 or higher receptivity to a fixed sentence. But as shown in Table 7, none of these relationships was sustained in a test of statistical significance.

Table 7
SUMMARY OF X^2'S

Independent Variable	N	Direction	X^2	Sig.
Year Founded	76	Institutions Built Before 1950> Than Institutions Built in 1950 and After	.9119	NS
Classification Systems	78	No Difference Between APA/Others vs. I-Level/Quay	.0173	NS
Size of Institution (population)	73	Small Institutions> Large Institutions	.394	NS
Release Methods	75	No Difference in Parole Board vs. Nonparole Boards	.219	NS
Cost Per Day for Institutional Care	61	High Costs> Than Low Cost	.384	NS

Agency and professional support of the indeterminate sentence appears intense (see Table 8). Only three percent of the superintendents varied from their agency's position when asked if they would abolish the indeterminate sentence in cases of involuntary commitments. Eighty-five percent of professionals rejected a change in public policy. Only 45 percent of the superintendents supported experimenting with the fixed sentence. Professionally, 67 percent of the respondents accepted removing status offenders from the juvenile correctional system. Agencies appeared less inclined (50 percent) in this direction.

Table 8

PERCENT OF SUPERINTENDENTS ENDORSING
THE FOLLOWING QUESTIONS

Questions	Percent Endorsing
1. Do you professionally endorse abolish- ing the indeterminate sentence in cases of involuntary commitments?	15%
Your agency's position?	12%
2. Would you support experimenting with the fixed sentence in your agency?	45%
3. Do you professionally advocate removing the status offender from the juvenile correctional system?	67%
Your agency's position?	50%

Toward Differentiation

Notwithstanding the limited sample, this survey strongly rejects the contention that juvenile correctional superintendents will be receptive toward establishing statutory sentences for the juvenile offender. Even when taking into account institutional factors, a majority of fixed sentence endorsements were found only in the category of "armed robbery." However, a relatively high proportion (67 percent) supported removing the status offender from the juvenile correctional system.

It is apparent that these respondents equated the fixed sentence with punishment, in that the more serious FBI-index offenses, i.e., homicide and armed robbery, elicited a higher endorsement than minor and status offenses. Therefore, from a public policy strategy point of view, it may be wise for supporters of the determinate sentence to initiate a legal and programmatic separation of the status offenders from the juvenile correctional system. In this respect, a superintendent from Iowa offered the comment:

> Children in need of supervision (status offenders) obviously should be in some other form of helping type of system. At the present time, we do not have that system in Iowa, but through reorganization, we are making studies toward developing local programs to take care of this type of offender.[3]

Following this measure, correctional administrators may be more inclined to support a statutory sentence for the juvenile offender linked to the gravity of the committing offense. Perhaps what is also required on a national level is an effort by a professional group to develop a "Model Sentencing Act for Juveniles" analogous to what the National Council on Crime and Delinquency formulated for the adult offender in 1963.[4] These recommendations and other social-policy implications will be elaborated upon in the following chapters.

7
PINS: DILEMMAS OF DECRIMINALIZATION

One of the most significant developments in juvenile law is the introduction of legislation prohibiting the institutionalization of individuals involved in "behavior illegal only for a child."[1] A modification of PINS or CINS (person/child in need of supervision) statutes, these provisions specifically set forth criteria and procedure for coercive* action to be taken against nondelinquent minors by the Juvenile Court and delegate agencies. Whether the adoption of and enforcement of these new laws will be in the best interest of the child and the community has yet to be determined. From a national policy point of view, it is incumbent upon us to review the assumptions and results of both existing and new PINS legislation before we commit ourselves to a given strategy of decriminalization. While the juvenile justice system is seen as a dismal failure, the

---

*This term refers to measures taken "against the will" of a child/parent to effect compliance of a court disposition.

anticipated and unanticipated consequences of an attractive solution may ultimately prove to be more of a threat than a contribution to the cause of "children's rights."

Children in Trouble: Two Definitions

There are two kinds of "children in trouble." The first is the child accused of an act that would be criminal if he were an adult. Statutes describe the prohibited behavior in rather precise language (e.g., robbery, aggravated assault) and violation subjects the juvenile to punishment such as probation or confinement. The second and more obscure category is those youth who exhibit uniquely juvenile misbehavior. Because of its importance in the evolution of PINS legislation, this chapter is concerned with the latter classification.

> ... While not charged with violations of the criminal law, [he] is accused of being 'beyond control', 'incorrigible', or 'ungovernable' and is deemed to be in need of restraints and sanctions similar or identical to those imposed on the child who is accused of a criminal offense.[2]

Nationally 41 states permit a juvenile to be adjudged a delinquent if he is found ungovernable or is guilty of immoral conduct. Fifteen states make incorrigibility the grounds for delinquency.[3] Because these states consolidate "uniquely juvenile" and "delinquent" conduct, they are called "single-statute" jurisdictions. The court can impose the same restraints and sanctions on both classes of offenders.[4] This accounts for the current integration of PINS-type children with delinquents in many of our training schools. In "separate-statute" jurisdictions, where states have attempted to distinguish between PINS and delinquent youth, the programs have not necessarily changed.

> In jurisdictions where PINS statutory provisions are separate from the delinquency, the PINS proceedings, although they are technically quasi-criminal and do not adjudge the juvenile a 'delinquent', still expose the child to similar or identical sanctions and label him a 'person in need of supervision'.[5]

Before discussing these observations and the possible outcome of recently adopted PINS provisions, some examples of general and revised PINS laws and related assumptions will be presented.

Person in Need of Supervision

The following paragraphs typify conduct that fall under "separate" PINS provisions. The New York Family Court Act (1963) defines a "person in need of supervision":

> A male less than 16 years of age and a female less than 18 years of age who is an habitual truant and who is incorrigible, ungovernable or habitually disobedient and beyond the lawful control of parent or other lawful authority.[6]

The Illinois Juvenile Court Act (1966) creates the category of "minor otherwise in need of supervision" (for reasons other than delinquency):

> a) Any minor under 18 years of age who is beyond the control of his parents, guardian, or other custodian and
> b) Any minor subject to compulsory school attendance who is habitually truant from school.[7]

A "child in need of supervision" under Maryland law means:

> A child (under 18 years) who requires guidance, treatment, or rehabilitation and:
> 1) is required by law to attend school and who is habitually truant from school;
> 2) is habitually disobedient, ungovernable, and beyond control of the person having custody of him without substantial fault on the part of that person;
> 3) deports himself so as to injure or endanger himself or others;
> 4) has committed an offense applicable only to children.[8]

Some bifurcated systems adjudicate a PINS child "delinquent" after a second PINS offense (e.g., Washington, D.C.) or if he fails to obey a court order (e.g., California).[9]

Recently PINS provisions have been modified to include

guidelines for detention and institutionalization. Effective January 1975 in Maryland:

> Detention is permitted only when a person is alleged or adjudicated to be a delinquent child ... a child alleged to be neglected, dependent, or *in need of supervision may not be placed in detention,* but only in shelter care facilities maintained by the Department of Social Services or any home or facility maintained by the Department of Juvenile Services for the child in need of supervision. [Section 3-832, italics added].[10]

Section 3-832 further instructs the court:

> If a child is found to be neglected, in need of supervision, mentally handicapped, or dependent, *the court may not confine the child in a juvenile training school or any similar institution* [italics added].[11]

We will now examine the assumptions of "the person in need of supervision" classification.

Assumptions of PINS

The history of PINS is marked with contradictions. It appears to have gone through three phases: humanitarian, decriminalization, and deinstitutionalization. While the first separate-statute PINS sections were adopted in the early sixties, it must be remembered that "uniquely juvenile" offenders now defined as PINS have been routinely dealt with by the juvenile court since its founding (1899). Thus to a significant degree, PINS provisions have always reflected the goals of social defense.

The first—"humanitarian"—era began in 1899 and lasted until 1962. It was characterized by the strong belief in the ability of social and behavioral science to rehabilitate juvenile offenders. During this period, social-defense strategies of probation, detention, and incarceration were employed against children accused of exhibiting "uniquely juvenile" behavior without regard to constitutional rights. In "the name of beneficence" nonconforming youth were expeditiously removed from the community and given the same "treatment" accorded delinquents. The assumption was that there was no acceptable community alternative, and like delinquents, these youths could benefit from juvenile court supervision and correctional programs.[12]

The second phase of PINS, falling between 1963 and the present, emphasized "decriminalization." During this time there was a growing consensus among certain lawmakers and social scientists that the term *juvenile delinquent,* in the eyes of the public, connoted criminal behavior and retribution. Consequently, antisocial children who did not commit criminal acts, were being falsely labeled. It was assumed that if the "uniquely juvenile" group was declassified "delinquent" vis-à-vis PINS, destigmatization and, hence, decriminalization would result. Contrary to popular belief, this was nothing more than a delabeling exercise. The relationship of the "uniquely juvenile" child to the juvenile court and correctional agencies did not change. Separate "treatment" and diversion were not at issue here.[13]

Admittedly, the assumptions of humanitarianism and decriminalization continue to operate as major themes or goals in the evolution of PINS and juvenile law. However, the most important change in PINS law is seen in the "deinstitutionalization" clause of state (Maryland) statutes. To adequately understand the assumptions of this development it is helpful to review the events which, in my estimation, set the conditions for such "deinstitutionalization-oriented" PINS laws. Although they do not pertain to PINS cases per se, taken together three Supreme Court decisions had a profound impact on the public's attitude toward the juvenile justice process and on the modes of entry into juvenile institutions.

Kent-Gault-Winship Trilogy

The Kent-Gault-Winship Supreme Court decisions revolutionized the juvenile court. Kent represents the first case to extend the constitutional protection of due process to juveniles.

[It] characterized the juvenile's predicament as 'the worst of both worlds' because there was evidence that he received neither the protections accorded adults nor the solicitous care and regenerative treatment postulated for children. *Kent* . . . invalidated a waiver order by which a juvenile accused of a serious crime was transferred to adult criminal court without a statement of reasons, a hearing, or effective assistance of counsel.[14]

In re Gault directly assaulted the principle of "parens patriae" as a "murky concept . . . of dubious relevance." (Gerald Gault was a 15-year-old resident of Arizona adjudicated a delinquent and institutionalized indefinitely for allegedly making obscene telephone calls.) The court held that the following due process guarantees were required in a delinquency proceeding which could result in confinement in a state institution:

1) adequate notice to parent and child . . . of the charge; 2) right to counsel; 3) privilege against self-incrimination; and 4) right to confrontation and cross-examination of witness.[15]

Finally *In re Winship* "held that proof must be 'beyond a reasonable doubt' before a juvenile could be adjudicated a delinquent for an act which would constitute a crime if committed by an adult."[16]

The above decisions add up to a blanket indictment of America's juvenile justice system. It forced unprecedented structural changes on the juvenile court and confirmed the fact that confinement in a training school constitutes punishment and deprivation of individual liberty. In essence, it laid the groundwork for dismantling the therapeutic state as far as controlling delinquency is concerned. In this respect, recent PINS revisions may be perceived as a last-ditch effort by those in disaccord with the Supreme Court to save the therapeutic state. On the other hand, it may represent a sincere humanitarian effort by children's-rights advocates to create community alternatives for youth accused of noncriminal conduct.

Implications of Deinstitutionalization

Proponents of the therapeutic state have long been at odds with extending constitutionalism to children and other social "misfits." The implication of abolishing coercive treatment is a threat to their working environment and their preconceived notions of man and behavior. The record shows that PINS legislation has not always met its expectations of decriminalization and deinstitutionalization. More ominously, there is reason to suspect that new PINS statutes may be used to circumvent constitutional protections granted accused delinquents and thereby shore up the therapeutic state. That is, if we compare the goals and assumptions of these PINS laws against what has actually transpired, the following hypotheses would emerge.

Projected Social Consequences

In this section, I will present hypotheses on the outcome of revised PINS laws derived from its major assumptions and from the findings of past research. A discussion of the research findings supporting the hypotheses and definitions will follow each statement. Parenthetically, we may anticipate that PINS laws will affect all of the components of the criminal justice system (e.g., police, court, corrections) and that these components will react differently according to community characteristics and the time PINS was enacted.

The first series of hypotheses will address the issue of decriminalization. This concept may be defined in various ways. It may be considered the degree to which each component of the criminal justice system, e.g., police, juvenile services intake, court, does not refer PINS youth to the next level of intervention. It may be seen as the extent to which PINS youth experience negative sanctions in the criminal justice system "before" and "after" PINS deinstitutionalization provisions. Viewed as a continuum, the lowest degree of decriminalization—most severe sanction—would appear in the category of training school commitment. The highest degree would be seen as a police contact only. Ideally, the new policy will produce higher rates of decriminalization. In this regard, research suggests that the central issue of recent PINS legislation is not diversion.

Rather, the focus should be on "who" will be diverted and "where"?

Hypothesis I (Diversion):

Diversion will be related to new PINS policy: at all stages of the criminal justice system it will be related to race (white), sex (male), and social class (nonpoor).

There is considerable evidence that the modes of entry (police, juvenile intake, court) into the criminal justice system are rigged against the poor, females, and minorities. That is, if we hold the legal factors (e.g., reason for referral or exhibited behavior) constant, the nonlegal factors (e.g., race, sex, social class) will predict diversion. Thornberry found this pattern in his study of sentencing practices in Philadelphia.[17] Sumner found evidence that nonlegal factors influence detention rates in California counties:

Fifty-four percent of those children with a prior record were detained in high-rate counties, contrasted with 23 percent (less than one-half as many) in the low-rate counties. . . .[18]

Sumner also concluded that "children classified as white were less likely to be detained."[19]

Discriminatory practices at the disposition stage was evident in New York's application of PINS statutes. The New York Office of Children's Services Policy Committee found that:

Twenty-four percent of the black and 24 percent of the Puerto Rican [PINS] children were placed in training schools in contrast with only 12 percent of the white children so placed.[20]

The effect of race on placement disposition of PINS children is presented in Table 1.

This investigator found that female status offenders have a higher probability of being institutionalized in a state training school than their male counterparts. For example, in Ohio a majority of incarcerated girls are committed on noncriminal acts. This compared to less than 20 percent for the males in this category.[21]

Table 1

PLACEMENT DISTRIBUTION OF
316 PINS CHILDREN BY ETHNIC BACKGROUND

Placement	Black	Puerto Rican	White	Other	Total
Social Services	27%	18%	5%	20%	19%
Training Schools	24	23	12		20
Voluntary Agencies	49	59	83	80	61
Total	100	100	100	100	100

SOURCE: *The PINS Child, A Plethora of Problems* (New York: Office of Children's Services, State of New York, November, 1973), p. 62.

Hypothesis II (Decriminalization):
Given reduced PINS commitments to state training schools or camps, there will be a significant increase in the use of "informal probation" against PINS youth.

There is reason to expect that where state agencies are enjoined from incarcerating PINS the court will be under greater pressure to resort to "informal probation" and official probation as a means of retaining social control over these youth. According to Stiller and Elder writing in *The American Criminal Law Review*:

. . . Since PINS children, like delinquents, have misbehaved or committed some offense against society, some courts have upheld regulations permitting them to be treated more harshly than dependent or neglected children.[22]

This further suggests a subhypothesis:
Hypothesis IIA (Decriminalization):
There will be a greater use of "violation of court order" and denial of procedural rights by the court to facilitate direct PINS commitments to training schools.

This hypothesis can be operationalized by comparing the use of counsel and formal adjudication procedures granted to

PINS "before" and "after" deinstitutionalization clauses. The same would apply to the issue of contempt citations to PINS for the purpose of incarceration. The potential for this type of abuse and related negative consequences is again underscored by Stiller and Elder:

> ... Such rights as notification of specific charges, representation by counsel, and confrontation and cross-examination of witnesses have not been held applicable to juvenile hearings where a PINS adjudication could result, often because such hearings are labelled non criminal proceedings.[23]
>
> ... Although it has been indicated that the mere possibility of eventual confinement does not raise this non criminal adjudication to the level of a delinquency hearing where incarceration can result, ... it may be argued that PINS children may ultimately be incarcerated or adjudicated delinquent and that this incarceration is a direct result of the original PINS adjudication.[24]

The anticipated consequences of deinstitutionalization policy on PINS youth will be mixed and somewhat difficult to evaluate.

Hypothesis III (Deinstitutionalization):
> Modified PINS legislation will be related to: a) a lower-rate institutionalization of uniquely juvenile offenders in training school and correction camps; b) a higher rate of institutionalization in public social-service shelter-care and foster homes; c) no difference in utilization rate of voluntary agencies.

These projections are drawn from the findings of a PINS impact study in New York. Court decisions prohibiting the commingling of PINS children with delinquents successfully reversed training school placements, but it did not alter the role of voluntary agencies. "While the voluntary agencies now provide care for a larger percentage of the PINS children, the total number accepted by those agencies from the court has remained virtually static." (See Table 2).[25]

According to the report "the number placed with the Commissioner of Social Services and maintained for months in temporary shelters increased sharply; the number returned to

Table 2

PLACEMENT OF PINS CHILDREN,
CALENDAR YEARS 1970, 1971, 1972

Placement	1970	1971	1972
Training Schools	482	295	99
Voluntary Agencies	345	357	374
Social Services	95	145	116
Total	922	797	589

SOURCE: *Ibid.*

destructive environments and rejecting parents also increased sharply."[26]

The report also stressed that specialized and scarce placements, such as residential treatment centers, went to whites. "It was secured for almost 63 percent of the white children for whom it was recommended as opposed to only 10 percent of the black and 9 percent of the Puerto Rican [PINS] children."[27]

If the above predictions hold, we may speculate that deinstitutionalization PINS policy will result in a significant number of lower-income and minority youth exchanging coercive placements or being transferred from one therapeutic state to another. In addition, we may anticipate that in the absence of adequate "noncoercive" private (voluntary) or public social services, a significant number of these children with serious behavior problems will be ignored. Depending on one's point of view, this may be a "mixed blessing." From these preliminary findings, there is very little evidence to support a position that revised PINS statutes will significantly divert poor and minority "persons in need of supervision" to first-rate noncoercive private agencies. The analysis will now turn to reviewing the "unanticipated" consequences of modified PINS laws.

The Unanticipated Consequences

Where the population of institutions has decreased because of the loss of PINS offenders, longer sentences are projected for those "delinquent" offenders left behind.

Hypothesis IV (Deinstitutionalization):
Modified PINS statutes will be associated with longer sentences for delinquent offenders.

As institution population is reduced and made up of more serious offenders, there is a strong possibility that more sophisticated "treatment" techniques will be introduced or revitalized in these settings. Consequently length of confinement will be extended to permit experimentation. This phenomenon is a function of the indeterminate sentence at work in "small" institutions. Nationally it is observed that longer institution stay is associated with small institutions that use advanced psychological classification systems (e.g., interpersonal maturity scale, Quay). Also, sentences will continue to be inequitable in that younger and least serious offenders will, as before PINS laws, experience equal or longer confinement than their older and more seriously delinquent counterparts.[28]

On the positive side there is evidence to suggest that youth classified as PINS who experience incarceration will exhibit a poorer community adjustment than their counterparts who are diverted from correctional facilities as a result of revised PINS laws.

Hypothesis V (Rehabilitation):
Youth who receive a PINS disposition "post"-revised PINS law will be less likely to become involved with the criminal justice system than "pre"-revised PINS law youth who were treated the same as delinquents (e.g. committed to training schools).

This projection stems from previous research, which shows that length of institution stay is positively related to recidivism.[29]

In summary, any future research effort directed at measuring the impact of modified PINS laws must determine: a) the extent to which it decriminalizes status offenses at the intake phase; b) the degree to which a PINS disposition keeps a youngster out of the correctional system and; c) the extent to which rehabilitative services for these PINS youth are better and less punitive than services afforded PINS youth before deinstitutionalization policies were implemented.

A Social-Policy Study: The Case of Maryland

Effective January 1975, Maryland law prohibited detaining or incarcerating PINS youth in facilities used for delinquents.[30] To evaluate the outcome of Maryland's new PINS law a comparative analysis of the status of PINS cases and related agencies "before" and "after" the adoption of this legislation is appropriate. For example, the "experimental" group would consist of a cohort sample of youth coming in contact with the police, the Department of Juvenile Services, and the Juvenile Court during the first three months of 1975. In addition to tracking the involvement of these subjects, we would examine significant organizational variables (e.g. treatment programs, population composition) of the community and correctional agencies utilized by these youth. The "control" group will be composed of two cohort samples of PINS cases disposed of at the police, the Department of Juvenile Services, and the Juvenile Court during the similar period in 1973 and 1974. The status of youth and agencies "before" and "after" the new PINS statute will be ascertained (see Figure 1). Significant client and agency variables will be compared over a five-year period (1973 through 1977).

Figure 1

LONGITUDINAL RESEARCH DESIGN

TIME 1	TIME 2	TIME 3
Before	New PINS Law	After
(1) 1973 cohort	(1) 1973 cohort	(1) 1973 cohort
(1) 1974 cohort	(1) 1974 cohort	(1) 1974 cohort
	(1) 1975 cohort	(1) 1975 cohort
		(1) 1976 cohort
		(1) 1977 cohort

Mode of Entry (impact variables)			Utilizations (outcome variables)	
Referring Agent:	Intake Factors:	Disposition	placement:	success vs.
Parents	Age	CINS vs. Delinq:	family	failure:
School	Sex	Police/Intake/Court	foster home	rearrest
Police	Race	dismissed	group home	reinsti.
	Income	informal prob.	institution	school dropout
	Arrest history	petitioned	detention	unemployed

In this design, the unit of analysis would be the cohort in relation to time and outcome in one or more component experiences in the criminal justice system. Cases would be examined and followed up from initial contact with the police, to the court and parole adjustment, if appropriate. The policy effect will also be determined by treating each organization phase or criminal justice component as a unit of analysis.

Policy and Program Implications

In terms of both policy formulations and effective program administration, knowledge of the "anticipated" and "unanticipated" consequences of new PINS legislation is imperative. It is particularly important to determine the conditions under which decriminalization- and deinstitutionalization-oriented legislation function successfully. Research suggests that unless procedural safeguards are taken to assure fair application of these policies, it may in effect only decriminalize the troubled children of the middle class. It may also discourage juvenile court monitoring and intervention in cases being mishandled or exploited by the private and public social-service sectors. Therefore, before we accept this version of PINS as reform legislation, it should be carefully evaluated. A longitudinal research design will facilitate this task.

8
THE CASE FOR NONCOERCIVE HUMANITARIANISM

> There must be a total retooling of the nation's therapeutic system—from custodial storehouses which suppress the skills of independent living into free therapeutic centers operating in the community and offering treatment to those who voluntarily seek it.
>
> Kittrie*

The purpose of this section is to clarify the relationship between rehabilitation and the indeterminate sentence. Abolition of the indeterminate sentence should not be interpreted as rejecting the principle of humanitarianism or rehabilitation. Such a conclusion, in my estimation, is without substance, belies professional training and ethics and is a direct assault on the imagination.

Two Views of Treatment Delivery

There is nothing to preclude the provision of job-training, education, and therapy programs for incarcerated offenders or individuals living in the community. The issue is the form of inducement: coercion versus self-determination. Does the state have the right to "change" a person against his or her will in

*Nicholas N. Kittrie, *The Right to Be Different* (Baltimore: Penguin Books, Inc., 1973), p. 101.

109

addition to depriving him or her of liberty? If the answer is no, and we are committed to humanitarianism, noncoercive helping strategies must follow. On the other hand, if we accept the position of imposing treatment on "captive clients," the argument is reduced to demonstrating an effective cure and safeguarding human rights. In view that compulsory rehabilitation has not demonstrated a cure[1], this point will be dismissed. However, an example of a juvenile residential institution, which employs safeguards against abuse of involuntary treatment, will be elaborated upon in this chapter.

Noncoercive Humanitarianism

Noncoercive humanitarianism is defined as the unconditional provision of noncompulsory rehabilitation services by a provider to an individual or group suffering problems in social functioning. Noncoercive humanitarianism can be operationalized in jails and the community. I will first discuss the merits and organization structure of this approach as it pertains to a typical adult prison population.

An average inmate has wants and needs not radically different from law-abiding citizens. Education and job training are perceived as important prerequisites to securing a legitimate livelihood. That incarcerated individuals often reject or "fail" such a program may be attributed to its irrelevancy to the real world (learning auto mechanics with an outdated engine and outdated tools) coupled to the fact that they are involuntary. To overcome this vacuum in program and lack of motivation, the noncoercive model allows inmates to become involved in developing and selecting courses consistent with their future career plans. Rather than depend solely on in-house instructional staff, correctional administrators are encouraged to contract educational, training, and housing services from the private and public sectors. Root observes:

> Most state programs have the option of contracting with county and city jails for the housing of work releases from state institutions. Use of such facilities permit a person to work in the vicinity of his house.[2]

For the correctional administrator, the pay-off will be seen in greater investment on the part of participants, less discipline problems, and better preparation of incarcerated offenders for today's job market. Since employers are beginning to view work releases' performance on the job as good or better than that of other workers, such options should not be overlooked.[3]

A similar case of contracting services can be made for the provision of bona fide therapy to inmates. When incarcerated offenders desire group or individual treatment, the prison administration may seek out professionals in the community. To those critics who maintain that trained social workers, psychiatrists, and psychologists will not respond to the demand, this will cease to be a problem when client confidentiality is respected by prison authorities. Currently, institutional treatment staff are agents of the parole board or the administration. Diagnostic impressions are often kept from the client and information obtained in therapy sessions is used against him. This presents a serious ethical problem for professionals. If the correctional administration or the court desires a psychiatric evaluation to make a program decision, it should recruit a professional specifically for this purpose, e.g., court-appointed psychiatrist. The offender in question should have the same right.

Lessons from the Counterculture

Some professionals contend that institutionalization and the indeterminate sentence are necessary because a significant number of offenders will not elect to engage in the treatment process in the community or during confinement. They are forced to take their medicine as a condition of release. This observation is accurate in the sense that people suffering various social problems are rejecting established agencies and related helping modalities. Witness the birth of counterculture services in the sixties, e.g., free stores, free clinics. People, who postponed contact with traditional helping agencies out of fear or distrust, flocked to these store-front aid stations.[4] Upon receiving assistance, some individuals stayed and worked as volunteers. Others went on to organize alternative human-service agencies in their neighborhood. By 1972, there were over 250 free clinic operations across the country serving 1.5 million people a year.[5]

Contrary to popular belief these alternative institutions are not just utilized by the "hippie" or "tuned-out" generation. Retired people, middleclass professionals, and low-income, minorities, and blue-collar workers seek help with no less vigor than "long-hair" youth on the run, drug-abuse victims, parolees, and women with problem pregnancies. While attracted to the free access to vital services, clients are equally lured by the egalitarian philosophy and democratic administration of these agencies. It is not uncommon for consumers of free clinics to donate money. Also, people suffering health problems, covered by third-party medical insurance went out of their way to receive treatment at clinics associated with the counterculture.[6]

The implications of this noncoercive treatment model do not go unappreciated by public health officials and elected representatives. In Los Angeles, the free clinics have received assistance since 1969. In awarding the Los Angeles and Long Beach Free Clinics each an $18,500 grant in drugs and supplies, the Los Angeles County Board of Supervisors reported:

> [Free] clinics have had an unusual degree of success not shared by public clinics in inducing certain groups of people in L.A. County who are likely to have such diseases to submit themselves for proper medical treatment and care, and have, therefore, been of material assistance in the performance of County's public health duties. . . .[7]

Three years later, the federal government's Health, Education, and Welfare (H.E.W.) gave direct financial aid to the free clinic.[8]

The Social-Change Model

Organizationally, the counterculture institutions fall in the nontraditional, social-change, "conflict" category (see Table 1).

Writing in *Community Problem Solving: the Delinquency Example,* Irving Spergel offers two orientation models of organizational influence and corresponding goals and structure: the social-stability and social-change model. These models are derived from each organization's strategic orientation to its social environment, which are "principally a resultant of two variables—goals, and decision-making." "The worker roles are largely determined by the interaction of these two variables."[9]

> Goals of service organization or community work organizations may be part of a continuum of directed social change and social stability. Each organization perceives, evaluates, and seeks to interact with its social environment. It may strive for large-scale, radical changes in institutional patterns that are regarded as basically defective. It may even urge revolutionary changes in the structure and purpose of other organizations. On the other hand, it may regard this present system as generally desirable and seek only slight changes in policies. . . . Then the organization's primary orientation is to maintain, and more effectively control the existing pattern of relationship in the society.[10]

Table 1
TYPES OF ORGANIZATIONAL ORIENTATION
AND STRATEGY

Organizational Structure	Organization Goal and Strategy	
	Social Stability	Social Change
Traditional	Maintenance	Contest
Nontraditional	Development	Conflict

Source: Irving A. Spergel, *Community Problem Solving: the Delinquency Example* (Chicago: University of Chicago Press, 1969), pp. 31-32.

The organization's orientation dictates the primary organizational strategy. There are four categories of organizational strategy: 1) maintenance, 2) development, 3) contest, and 4) conflict. *Maintenance* is characterized by a conservative and authoritarian approach to achieving incremental progress. Policy and program is controlled by the elite or professional groups. Spergel reports that most organizations use this approach. These will include the welfare and criminal justice systems, large corporations, and established labor unions. The *development* strategy is typified by minority-group programs of limited resources that strive for indigenous cultural building in attempts to solve local problems. This strategy is directed toward protecting the groups' limited gains against expansion programs of the dominant culture and depredations of deviant members of the community. Its strategy tends to be conservative and the leader autocratic and paternalistic. We will expect ethnic-oriented communities to rely on these tactics. *Contest* is a strategy of intervention characterized by an elite or professional group advocating social policies and programs that seek to change existing institutional patterns. Its methods are legally sanctioned and approved by norms of a democratic society. Action is carried on in a respectable and restrained manner. The National Association of Social Workers fall in this category. *Conflict* strategy is exemplified in the organization's insistence on radical modification of existing institutional programs including the decision-making pattern for allocating and developing new resources. The Welfare Rights Organization is an example of this orientation and strategy.[11]

If an innovative noncoercive voluntary organization employing conflict strategy can effectively overcome a client boycott of services in the health field, it may be equally applicable to preventing or reducing crime and delinquency. The likelihood of reinvesting in grassroots community-action programs in high crime-rate areas however appears dim. They constitute a serious threat in terms of funds and power to traditional maintenance organizations, which continue to monopolize the criminal justice system. This brings us to the question of involuntary treatment of incarcerated juveniles.

Involuntary Treatment of Incarcerated Juvenile Offenders

The vast majority of confined juvenile offenders can effectively be supervised in the community with the assistance of negative sanctions. Nonviolent offenders can be given citations or ticketed for transgressions with proportionate fines or work assignments in the community.[12] The advantage of the negative sanction or "creative punishment" is making the offender immediately accountable for his illegal behavior. It also avoids imputing the "sick" role to young lawbreakers. This concept will be further discussed in Chapter 9.

To those bent on imposing treatment in residential programs for juvenile offenders, there are procedural and organizational safeguards available to reduce abuse. The first step is to separate the older street criminal from youth disposed to acting out against authority figures and peers. In contrast to those who use weapons and threaten people with violence, this youngster is a chronic but impulsive fighter. Also inclined to destroy property without provocation, he is generally unresponsive to external controls at home or in the community. Statistically this group makes up less than 5 percent of the delinquent population. Acknowledging that this youngster must be held accountable for his unlawful behavior, he does not warrant a locked cell or security-oriented program. Neither should he, as is often the case, be given institutional priority over the dangerous felon. The following is an example of one county's attempt to positively construct a program for the acting-out youngster.

Camp Kilpatrick: Approaching the Ideal Type

Rehabilitation in most juvenile correctional institutions is a sham and counterproductive. Notwithstanding radical change in social policy, America will continue to rely on the public sector to cope with delinquency. Therefore, for the sake of optimism and possible generalization, locating an "ideal type" in the public sector is appropriate.

Camp Vernon Kilpatrick is a residential setting operated by the Los Angeles County Probation Department. Located on top of the Santa Monica mountains, it is designed to house ninety-five "emotionally disturbed" and "aggressive" young adolescent boys, ages 12 to 16. Its accommodations include two forty-boy open-ward dorms and one twenty-boy orientation unit with individual private rooms. The camp has twenty-one counselors. All are college trained, work 62 consecutive-hour shifts and carry a case load between two and five boys. The facility also has a full-time school program. Placement is restricted to one year by the juvenile court. The average stay is seven months.*

Camp Kilpatrick was created in the early 1960's to cope with the most acting-out youngsters coming through the Los Angeles County juvenile court. Residents are characterized as hostile, aggressive, and suffering from severe feelings of rejection and poor peer relationships. In the home or community their anger has the effect of a tidal wave hitting an insecure beachhead, moving with great thrust and destroying everything in its path. Their court records are replete with destruction-of-property offenses, assault, and runaway.

In philosophy, organization structure, and program, Camp Kilpatrick is unique. Except for extreme physical violence or suicidal tendencies, residents are not threatened with transfer to another institution or to the California Youth Authority. This policy fosters an attitude of total staff commitment to each resident and confirms his ability to succeed in the program. Unless laws are broken in the community, running away from camp is not seen as a conspiracy against the institution. It is expected and seldom costs the culprit "extra days." Although physical force is used to restrain an acting-out youth, slapping or hitting a youngster in response to physical or verbal abuse is prohibited, and this prohibition is strictly adhered to. Marching is also against policy as is group punishment.

Organizationally, a counselor is expected to participate in all aspects of camp life. He carries an individual- and group-counseling case load. He is responsible for direct supervision of the dormitory, organizing on- and off-campus recreation, assisting in education, and sharing kitchen patrol (KP) and campus maintenance and cleanup. The facility has no guards or private offices. Except for the director, teachers, and secretaries everyone eats and sleeps on the grounds. Administratively, the

---

*This represents a limited version of the indeterminate sentence which I continue to oppose. In my two years of counseling experience here, no one's stay was extended beyond one year, and it was not uncommon for staff to give a youngster his release date long in advance.

functions of rehabilitation and supervision are formally and informally integrated along relatively horizontal hierarchical lines.

The impact of the organization structure on staff-student relationship is profound. Living with residents, staff are exposed to and compelled to work through mutual conflicts, depression, and anxiety. To avert boredom and survive isolation, boys and staff must be resourceful. Concrete rewards for achieving in school and talking rather than acting out a problem are only limited by imagination. Activities include hiking, beach outings, arts and crafts, model building, physical fitness, golf, Ping-Pong, and pool. Finally, because the unusual "fireman's hours" attract counselors who have a strong sense of independence, scepticism toward authority, and respect for personal freedom, there is little inclination to stress conformity. The net result is high esprit de corps, minimal turnover, and an institutional culture, which shuns staff exploitation of residents or each other. Thus the best safeguard against instilling an "us versus them" attitude and "sick/bad" client role is to formally create conditions that maximize staff-resident empathy. This is achieved in Kilpatrick by requiring staff and students to live together and not separating treatment from supervision. But to truly emerge into an "ideal-type" correctional facility, Camp Kilpatrick must totally discard the philosophy of the indeterminate sentence and participation in treatment as an incentive for release. Such a radical change in policy would not significantly undermine staff authority or result in a drastic role adjustment. Kilpatrick personnel are already involved in developing voluntary helping or "treatment" programs. They assist residents in planning "voluntary" recreation activities and exploring educational and training options. Counselors also work with interested parents and relatives on scheduling home visits and special events in the institution and community. A "flat" sentence may initially threaten staff who lack confidence in their ability to establish a trusting relationship with youth under their supervision. After all, before assignment to Camp Kilpatrick, many counselors have had no professional training in noncoercive rehabilitation techniques. It is primarily through the residential experience itself that noncoercive skills are acquired. Regardless of the indefinite nature of the residents' institutional stay, learning voluntary-counseling skills is necessary for developing effective working relationships with camp residents. Moreover, it is also made necessary by administrative dictates that Kilpatrick staff seek alternatives to the threat and use of physical punishment. This policy is enforced to the extent that residents are not permitted to be assaulted by staff in anger, handcuffed to bedposts, forced to march, or placed in a solitary cell. That the camp's personnel eventually adapt to nonviolent strategies in working with extremely acting-out youth is not attributed to administrative policy alone. It is soon learned by both staff and residents that it is humanly impossible to negotiate a 62-hour shift in either an atmosphere of lockstep repression or the unmitigated disorder that accompanies permissive indifference.

Notwithstanding the pressure from an enlightened hierarchy, the fact that Camp Kilpatrick counselors adopted noncoercive helping strategies suggest that, given a similar administrative dictate—to cease and desist indeterminate sentencing and forced therapy—they would make an equally constructive effort to comply. Because the Kilpatrick "ideal-type" (live-in) organizational structure fosters staff/resident empathy, we can predict that counselors would adapt satisfactorily to an offense-determined "fixed" stay. This is so because, under the present policy of the indeterminate sentence, counseling or treatment is rarely forced or viewed as a separate function within the total program. Within a three-day around-the-clock shift, duties are evenly distributed among staff and residents, relationships are encouraged, and problems are resolved. A "treatment session" may consist of talking an angry and frightened youth down from a tree or off a high fence, planning a hike or umpiring a staff/resident baseball game. If for some unexplicable reason, a busload of M.S.W.'s, Ph.D.'s, or otherwise trained therapists suddenly arrived on the Kilpatrick grounds to conduct conventional treatment, it is rather doubtful that many youngsters would elect to participate. But if the therapist offered to take a group fishing off Malibu Pier or supervise a youth on a home visit, they would have some takers. The strength of the Kilpatrick model lies in its capacity to operationalize a "fixed" sentence without sacrificing its humanistic residential life-style. If Camp Kilpatrick divested itself of the indeterminate sentence today, it would be in my estimation an "ideal-type" correctional setting. It would be "ideal," not as a "treatment" model (no one has demonstrated a curative model), but as a "humanitarian-oriented" facility.

The Kilpatrick philosophy and organizational structure stands in sharp contrast to most public residential settings best described as warehouses for children. They have evolved into oppressive instruments of self-serving interest groups, e.g., patronage dispensers, union organizers, and professional elites, who find comfort in perpetuating the treatment/custody organizational dichotomy. The actors have long internalized the fringe benefits of the "therapeutic state": guaranteed salary upgrades provided through creeping-step raises, eternal one-upmanship over the most vulnerable client group, lack of competition inherent in monolithic power, and the security built in the luxury of nonaccountability and public indifference. In the future, we can count on these groups to fight any attempt to abolish the indeterminate sentence. To them it has been the most important vehicle for covering incompetence, hiding brutality, and promoting lockstep conformity.

In summary, subjecting offenders to compulsory-treatment programs is an affront to our human and democratic values. It reduces man to an object of manipulation. It not only aims to change man externally but internally; in essence it attacks man's spiritual quality. In addition to being a moral outrage, treatment "under duress" does not significantly reduce crime or delinquency. Therefore, using the indeterminate sentence to compel people to participate in an unproven treatment process as a condition of freedom is needless and reprehensible. Noncoercive strategies are available to assure the retention of human values in the absence of the indeterminate sentence.

These include offering incarcerated offenders the opportunity to accept or reject counseling without prejudice. Where appropriate, correctional administrators may contract for specialized services without compromising client confidentiality. The initial hope of employing noncoercive helping strategies lies in the social-change "conflict-type" organization based in the community. As exhibited in the free clinics associated with the counterculture movement, people suffering from psychosocial disorders—who reject conventional help—will voluntarily respond to assistance. The social-change model also has the advantage of helping the socially and economically deprived deal more effectively with the institutions that dominate their lives.

Finally, in situations that require the provision of treatment to confined youth, the best protection against abuse is to operationalize treatment and supervision (custody) under a single "rehabilitation" function. Administratively it is imperative to have qualified staff working around the clock and living with residents under their care. Comparatively, this organizational structure is no more costly than training schools that waste millions in producing inane paperwork, enforcing ludicrous security measures, and creating the fraudulent impression of rehabilitation. In the long view, the adoption of the philosophy of noncoercive humanitarianism hinges on the demystification of the "therapeutic state." With the aid of the computer and evaluation research, this is becoming a possibility. Until this happens, we will continue to be victims of the policies of counterdeterrence and prisoners of the "therapeutic state."

9
A NEW POLICY OF
JUVENILE JUSTICE

> Policy analysis . . . asks, not what is the
> cause of a problem, not what is the condition
> one wants to bring into being, but what
> measure do we have that will tell us when
> that condition exists, and finally what
> policy tools does a government (in our case,
> a democratic and libertarian government)
> possess that might, where applied, produce
> present condition or progress toward the
> desired condition?
>
> James Q. Wilson*

The juvenile justice system is a paradox. In the name of
benevolent intervention and rehabilitation, it has operationalized a sentencing and parole procedure that discriminates
against females, the young, and the least-serious offender.

Nationally, only 15 percent of the states recorded length
of institution stay by committing offense. In the majority that
reported this information, there was no significant difference
in the sentence of FBI-index and status offenses. A similar conclusion was made when organizational variables were examined. No significant variation was found on institution stay
across the country when controlling on institution population,
parole-board status and type of classification system used to di-
agnose delinquents. These findings seem to suggest that nation-

---

*James Q. Wilson, "Crime and Criminologists," *Commentary,* Vol. 58, No. 1,
July 1974.

ally we are employing a "fixed" sentence on the juvenile offender unrelated to committing offense.

To better ascertain the relationship between offender characteristics and length of incarceration and parole an indepth analysis of the sentencing practices of a large Midwestern state was made. Serious inequities were discovered. Long-term institutions formally identified as "treatment" facilities discriminated against whites in confinement. In addition there was no statistical evidence of "individualized" treatment, except for race and age, in the sentencing practices of institutions. Rather, sentencing appeared to be a function of a given institution's adaptation to the "revolving door" or a tendency to adjust to new admissions and manipulate population by releasing residents within a similar and predictable time frame extraneous to offender characteristics. In terms of outcome, incarceration was shown to be counterproductive in that length of stay was found positively related to recidivism.

In regard to parole, the juvenile justice system appears to have used the philosophy of the indeterminate sentence to extend the therapeutic state to the community. Like institution stay, we observed little relationship between committing offense and length of parole. However, there was a pattern of longer community supervision for the two youngest age categories (10-to-14 and 15 years) and black parolees. Also, in serious-offense categories, younger females received significantly shorter parole than their male counterparts. In reference to success, we observed that a third of the total number of youth released from institutions were returned. But examining the outcome in State X's individual parole regions, we found no relationship between parole duration and return rate. The vast majority of youth were returned on technical violations without a court hearing. Each region exhibited a unique pattern of parole supervision and revocation extraneous to the type of offender or community. In essence, parole regions functioned as semiautonomous units without benefit of a uniform standard or central policy.

These findings reject the major assumptions of the indeterminate sentence as it applies to "individualized" treatment in institutions and parole. On the contrary, the analysis showed that length of incarceration and parole are more a function of the personality of the institution and parole region than the individual characteristics of the offender. Where patterns of discrimination occurred (age, sex, and race) it was not explained by criminality. What this means is that the juvenile justice system is neither achieving its mission of rehabilitation or social control. More significant, in its relentless pursuit of the indeterminant sentence, it has abandoned the principle of justice for the nation's juveniles and fostered a policy of counterdeterrence that encourages crime.

The fact that felony-index offenders are treated equally or less punitively than home truants and minor offenders results in serious sentencing and parole inequities. It also assures a disproportionate application of correctional resources on youngsters who represent the least threat to the community. That is, the dangerous offenders are subject to less attention and may be prematurely released from the institution and given a short parole. Consequently, this group may receive the false impression that the criminal justice system, post conviction, is a cakewalk. This stems from the juvenile authorities' deemphasizing the behavior responsible for incarceration. (Of course, this impression will be quickly dispelled if or when a youth experiences the adult penal system.) Finally, the incentive to participate in criminal acts is increased for status and minor offenders because they are confronted by youth who have committed serious crime but who will be released as soon or sooner than themselves. This is an absurd form of justice and strategy to reduce crime, if not a direct assault on our moral sensibilities. A new policy of juvenile justice is required.

Parenthetically, survey results of juvenile institution administrators' attitude toward a "fixed" sentence offer little hope that correctional officials will take independent action to eliminate sentencing disparities and abuses related to the indeterminate sentence. Therefore, any specific public policy recommendations directed toward rationalizing the juvenile sen-

tencing structure and improving services must take into consideration the negative social consequences of discretionary
authority. That is, the intent of new policy must be to control
significant organizational input (e.g., type of offenders, personnel standards) and output variables (e.g., length of incarceration and parole). Furthermore, reforming the juvenile justice
system calls for the repudiation of correctional social policy
founded on the following undemocratic and unproven assumptions: first, that coercive humanitarianism or compulsory
rehabilitation reduces crime and delinquency; second, that
children and juveniles do not deserve justice; and thirdly, that
bona fide rehabilitation exists in correctional practices. Rejecting these assumptions we must be prepared to initiate social
policy that promotes the realization that young people are
capable of being responsible for their own actions. Ultimately,
new policy must be committed to dismantling the therapeutic
state as we know it.

Major Social-policy Recommendations

To effectively overthrow the therapeutic state and eliminate its related abuses, the following social-policy measures are
recommended:

1. Endorse noncoercive humanitarian philosophy and
practice in the administration of community agencies and institutions working with troubled youth.

To extend the noncoercive humanitarian mode of service
to potential and delinquent youth in the community, federal
and local assistance should be granted to nontraditional "social-
change-oriented" organizations. Analogous to the administrative guidelines of the Economic Opportunity Act, funding
should be predicated on representative participation of community, professional, and consumer groups (young people). It is
anticipated that such programs, in reflecting the values and
needs of youth, will attract those in trouble with the law or
established institutions. In this regard, like the counterculture-
type free health clinics, there should be total adherence to the
principle of confidentiality and no charge for service.

On a juvenile correctional-institution level, financial inducement should be made to administrators to replace the dichotomous treatment/custody table of organization with an integrated rehabilitation model (e.g. Camp Kilpatrick). This may be accomplished by state legislators adopting personnel standards for juvenile correctional agencies. This should be done in conjunction with adopting a "fixed" sentence linked to the gravity of the offense for the juvenile offender (see recommendation number 4). If we merely reorganize institutional staffing patterns, e.g., 62-hour shift, and raise personnel standards, e.g., college degree, but retain the indeterminate sentence, there will be minimal incentive to develop noncoercive rehabilitation programs. Sentencing disparity and "treatment" abuses will continue. However, if we fail to alter the organization structure or preserve the traditional treatment/custody dichotomy operation, many criminal justice critics will mistakenly perceive adopting a "fixed" sentence as a carte blanche sanction to further dehumanize our correctional institutions. Accepting the principle that lawbreakers should receive their "just deserts," does not mean relegating incarcerated individuals to an empty or hostile institutional experience. Punishment is achieved by removing the transgressor from his or her home and community.

In this regard, the Kilpatrick organization structure functions as a safeguard against abuses that may follow the implementation of a "fixed" sentence. A live-in college-trained staff will be disinclined to settle for a lockstep or dehumanized residential program. In this situation it is difficult for employees to manipulate their working environment to avoid personal relationships with residents and staff.

Under a "fixed" sentence a Kilpatrick-type institution will create noncoercive humanitarian treatment programs. It will appear in the form of voluntary recreation activity, spontaneous interaction inherent in residential living, mutual education planning, and optional individual and group counseling. For example, we may expect that a 14-year-old male youth sentenced to 90 days for repeated acts of purse snatching may reject traditional one-to-one casework counseling. However, it is highly unlikely that he will reject participating in recreation excursions off the institution grounds or staff-accompanied home visits. Also, there is no evidence that boys age 13 to 16 are reluctant to participate in youth-oriented residential-group work projects, e.g., photography, arts and crafts, organized sports, etc.

We may envisage a situation in which a discharged youth, not on parole (see recommendation number 5) who is experiencing difficulty in the community, will request returning to the institution for a weekend to talk out his problems with counseling staff who worked effectively with him previously. We may also see the day when public juvenile correctional settings offer financial incentives to parents of residents to spend a weekend at or near the institution for the purpose of visiting their children and involving themselves in family counseling. This strategy is working effectively in private residential facilities for children.[1] Ultimately, noncoercive treatment is a function of personal motivation and trust in the helping agent. Assuming that most people have a vested interest in improving their lot, counseling resources should be made freely available to those who want them, not on the grounds of "cure," but on the principle of "humanitarianism."

There is little basis for pessimism about providing non-coercive treatment in a correctional setting modeled upon Camp Kilpatrick and governed by a "fixed" sentence. Most professional practitioners are formally trained in noncoercive treatment methods. That so few trained clinicians are found in juvenile and adult correctional facilities today testifies to the repugnance of coercive treatment and unattractiveness of the custody/treatment organization structure. If public policy provided for confidential and voluntary therapy in juvenile and adult institutions, there is every indication that professionals, who would otherwise refuse to practice in these programs, will offer their services. Not the least disincentive to participation is officials' using information obtained in therapy sessions for parole decisions or a criteria of release. In regard to inmate attitude toward treatment, it should be noted that recent prison riots and prisoner-rights movements show that, in addition to wanting the abolition of the indeterminate sentence, e.g., Patuxent, inmates are demanding "more" not less (noncoercive) counseling services, e.g., Lorton.[2]

2. Employment of "creative" punitive sanctions other than incarceration for minor and nonviolent offenders.

Some state legislators have given the local police the authority to issue citations to juvenile law violators. "One of the interests of Maryland's Juvenile Code was to establish a screening and informal adjustment procedure to serve to divert minor antisocial instances from the formal court system and to substitute a period of informal counseling to parents and child in terms of the causes of such behavior and ways to deal with 'minor acting out' in the home and community."[3] Unfortunately, because of staff shortage in the Department of Juvenile Services, Maryland officials have observed a 4-to-6-weeks delay in handling misdemeanor kinds of offenses, e.g., loitering, trespassing, petty larceny, shoplifting, disorderly conduct, possession of alcohol, etc. Consequently, such behavior may be ignored or permitted to escalate until it results in incarceration.

As an alternative to this delay, Maryland's Anne Arundel County instituted a citation program under the informal adjustment provision of the juvenile code. According to one county official:

> This method rests on the hypothesis that the more immediate and firm the response to minor socially deviant behavior the greater the likelihood of altering juvenile behavior patterns. . . . A way to attain this would be to establish a system of swift and decisive responses to antisocial behavior of less serious nature. Such a structure should include expeditious responses by law enforcement officials in the form of citations (similar to adult tickets), followed by informal hearings with the Department of Juvenile Services within 3 days. This should be followed by redress of a constructive, visible nature within the community. For example, volunteer work in the schools, with the parks, or community helping agencies . . . and of greater significance, [it] involves the community itself in constructive rehabilitation of juveniles. . . .[4]

Referred to as the Community Arbitration Program, this concept was launched in the fall of 1973 with the aid of the Law Enforcement Assistance Administration. Heretofore the program has received considerable support from the community and especially the police. There has also been a strong inducement for the offender to participate:

> If the juvenile admits the offense and agrees to participate in the programs, he or she will have no record. If, however, the juvenile refuses the penalty and the case goes to court, a record could result.[5]

California law also offers a citation option to the local police.[6] Police citations have been used by the Fresno County Sheriff's Office for about 15 years. They divert about 80 percent of the youth from juvenile court. According to Merry Morash, who helped organize Maryland's citation program, this type of criminal sanction is successful because it drops off stigma. It also enhances the relationship between the police and the juvenile because the former act as an unofficial arbitrator between the street and the court.[7]

In Palo Alto, youths cited for minor violations are referred to the Community Youth Responsibility Program. Cases are heard before a quasi-judicial board made up of six young people. Disposition includes cleaning up the yards of houses offenders burglarized or in supervising children in a recreation center. The program has demonstrated a low 7 percent recidivism rate.[8]

A modification of the above "quick juvenile justice systems" is a point system analogous to traffic citations used in many states. Once a youth has accumulated a certain number of points (lose driver's license) a proportionate punitive sanction may be employed, e.g., official probation, weekend in jail, etc.

In the past, citation programs have been contingent on funding and community interest. At this juncture, it seems constructive for states to institute this mode of criminal sanction on a universal basis. Finally, the employment of juvenile citation programs is somewhat related to the recent trend of

"creative punishment" imposed by adult courts. In lieu of institutionalization, judges have sentenced certain convicted offenders to work in community service to "pay back" the community. A federal judge recently sentenced two Texas milk
producers to work with the poor as punishment for price fixing. In Miami, criminal court Judge Alfonso Sepe ordered a
young marijuana smuggler to go back to college, get a job, report his grades, and write a paper on whether marijuana has
harmful effects. "A youth convicted of disorderly conduct and
violently resisting arrest was required to teach a jail inmate
how to read."[9]

Recognizing that this practice still does not deal with the
problem of sentencing disparity, it represents a reasonable
trade-off to incarcerating nonviolent offenders. That is, while
"creative punishment," for the most part, will be determined
by the nature of the infraction, judges and community-arbitra-
tion-type boards will vary sentences for similar offenders. But
there is no reason not to formulate explicit policy directed
toward matching creative punishments in the community
with the offense itself.

3. Decriminalization of status offenses.

Delinquency is synonymous with crime. In most states
running away, school truancy, incorrigibility and curfew violation fall under delinquency. The result is criminalization of
thousands of young people who, except for age, would not be
labeled criminal. More important, these youngsters are co-
mingled with hardcore youthful felons in institutions and subjected to the same parole conditions. This policy also results in
overcriminalization of teenage girls who are disproportionately incarcerated on status offenses. The criminalization of
status offenders has evolved from the misleading image gener-
ated by juvenile correctional officialdom that their programs
are humane, rehabilitating, and devoid of punishment. These
officials have become victims of their own propaganda.

Diverting status offenders from the juvenile correctional
system is a complex problem. It not only calls for a clear and
legislative mandate to prohibit processing these youth as delin-

quents, it requires financial investment in community-based programs and imposing sanctions against discriminatory voluntary agencies. It also necessitates an effective monitoring of these programs by the juvenile court and legislators (see recommendation number 6) to avoid exploitation of clients and the public funds. Whatever the inconvenience to legislators, the courts, and the social-service network, anything less than a total commitment to decriminalize the status offenders is morally reprehensible.

4. Abolition of the indeterminate sentence.

Abuses associated with the indeterminate sentence cannot be exaggerated. Picture three college students with identical warts on the index finger. They all report to the same health clinic for treatment. The first student, by some fortunate chance of fate, is assigned to Dr. A. He elects to burn off the wart. The second student draws Dr. B. His prescription is removal of the index finger. The third student, for some unlucky reason, sees Dr. C. His solution is amputation of the arm. Do the above examples appear farfetched?

Federal Judge Marvin Frankel, writing in *Criminal Sentences: Law without Order*, states:

> The fashioning of sentences are terrifying and intolerable for a society that professes devotion to the rule of the law. For examples of such unbounded 'discretion' ... An assault upon a federal officer may be punishable by a fine and imprisonment for 'not more than ten years'. The federal kidnapping law authorizes 'imprisonment for any term of years or for life'. Rape ... leads to death, or 'imprisonment for any term of years or for life'.[10]

According to Frankel "this means in the great majority of federal criminal cases that a defendant who comes up for sentencing has no way of knowing or reliably predicting whether he will walk out of the court room on probation, or be locked up for a term of years that may consume the rest of his life or something in between."[11]

We have previously demonstrated sentencing abuses

experienced by juveniles subject to the "unbounded discretion" of institution staff. Length of stay for equivalent offenders ranged from 6 months to 2 years.

Our findings on the effects of "prisonization" also refute the theory that "treating" people against their will or subjecting incarcerated individuals to arbitrary rehabilitation programs, with equally arbitrary expectations, as a condition of release, reduces criminal behavior or delinquency. What was proven is that the indeterminate sentence is associated with abuse and inequities in sentencing. Therefore, from the standpoint of fairness and general deterrence, it is appropriate for the state legislatures to set sentences for juvenile offenses of a serious and felonious nature. Flexibility could be provided by granting the juvenile court authority to increase or lower a statutory "flat" sentence under special circumstances by 20 percent. In addition to abolishing parole and forced therapy, this guideline has been proposed for the adult correctional system by former Illinois Governor Walker.[12] The rationale for recommending that sentences be the primary responsibility of the legislature is to assure more uniformity in punishment and public involvement in the criminal justice process. But it must be recognized that institution staff have been no less arbitrary in dispensing rehabilitation (punishment) than the courts.

Adopting a flat sentence for offenses committed by juveniles should not be seen as threatening citation programs or creative punishment efforts. The criteria for incarceration should be restricted to violent offenders and habitual offenders. Under this proposal, the law will allow for incentive for lesser offenders to participate in community penance, e.g., option of a year of community work in a charitable organization in lieu of 90 days in jail or a $10,000 fine. In this case, the offender will elect his or her "just deserts" within the parameters spelled out in the statute. Obviously, for serious felonies there will be no alternative to incarceration for a "flat" sentence. We must remember that the essence of the "flat" sentence is punishment equity: the prisoner's right to know when he gets out of jail and the citizen's right to know what coercive action his government will take against people engaged in specific unlawful acts.

This recommendation also implies rejecting the current "right to (coercive) treatment" movement. This, in effect, is more "treater" than "treatee" oriented. That is, states may be enjoined to provide more "professional" staff in existing institutions to assure some notion of "treatment." If we recall the length-of-stay pattern of professionally dominated private residential settings, adopting the "right-to-treatment" philosophy may result in the right of administrators to prolong confinement of "captive clients" in remote, rural-based institutions, or a right to practice indiscriminate psychosurgery. This is not to suggest that residential programs should not be professionalized. It merely negates the principle that the judgment of professional elites is applicable to the fundamental issue of human freedom in a democratic society. Professional elites include judges, social workers, psychologists and psychiatrists. Such decisions must hinge on the rule of law determined by the elected representatives of the people, not the rule of rehabilitation or behavior theories.

5. Abolition of juvenile parole or aftercare.

Juvenile parole or aftercare extends the abuses of therapeutic state to the community. It neither reduces crime nor concentrates on policing the most dangerous offenders in the community. It seems clear from parole outcome studies that youth will be afforded more legal safeguards if re-arrested and tried than if returned to jail by a parole agent without a court hearing. In regard to rehabilitation, it appears more constructive to refer released youth to service brokers in the community without the stigma of parole.

Under the condition of a "fixed" sentence, authorities may consider making parole services optional. But in this arrangement the treater would have to assume responsibility for failure as well as success. Professor Leslie T. Wilkins observed that the released offender could take the risk:

(a) Not be "bugged" or suffer surveillance (i.e., "treatment"); or

(b) Take the "treatment" (surveillance) and receive credit (say 25 percent off punishment which falls under [a] above) if he got into trouble again. This seems fair since if a man seeks treatment, then the treaters are partly to blame if he/it fails ... he should not be punished for that failure![13]

The incentive (sentence reduction if treatment fails) could be variable so as not to overload the treatment facilities. Also the effectiveness of treatment could be measured using the level of participation in relation to reward. If the "risk" to the exoffender of volunteering is increased (lower sentence reduction) and he continues to voluntarily utilize service at the same or higher rate, it can be deduced that the treatment is working. Conversely, if the "risk" is decreased (higher sentence reduction) or held constant and there is a dropping off of volunteers, one might surmise that: (1) the reduced-sentence benefit is not considered great enough by exoffenders to overcome the cost of participating in the voluntary program (from an exoffender's point of view he may not feel a 5 percent versus 25 percent sentence reduction is worth the "risk" of failure): and (2) the treatment or cure is not working.

6. Mandatory computer monitoring and evaluation by state legislatures, juvenile courts, and federal granting agencies.

Dearden and Nolan report in the *Harvard Business Review* that the computer resource has a simple purpose—economy:

The computer resource exists solely to help staff offices and operating units to execute their responsibilities better through cheaper processing of data, more efficient organization of information systems, and procurement and deployment of information that is too expensive to obtain otherwise. The resource has no reason for existing, except to provide such services, and these services should result in greater profits. In short, the resource has a purely economic purpose.[14]

If this is so, how can a "profit" motive be translated into the operation of a public social-service organization such as a state correctional agency?

The business of government is providing essential services or activity as economically as possible. The utility of a computer resource is found in its ability to measure the cost-effectiveness of a given program. It achieves this by presenting an instant picture of the status quo. In addition, the computer functions as a tool for evaluation and planning. For example, a systems analyst is able to line up a set of variables to measure present program outcomes. He may also test outcomes, given past trends or alternative program conditions. Finally, because modern electronic data processing is able to analyze data at the speed of light the computer resource has the potential to revolutionize the correctional information system.

To facilitate the diligent gathering and analysis of information, state legislatures should create a federal-type nonpartisan General Accounting Office (GAO), independent of the executive and undue influence of the majority party. In the past, state legislative-accountability efforts have been impaired by staff shortages, preoccupation with providing legal technical support and political manipulation.[15]

Program monitoring and evaluation should also be intensified by federal granting agencies and the juvenile court. Progress reports should be standardized, reviewed by decision-makers, and made readily accessible to the public and news media. It is an accepted fact that we monitor or keep better "track" of our cars using turnpikes and the flow of oil and other "vital" resources than the status of the millions of children and youth placed outside the home by the courts and social agencies. Is it not time the nation appoint a human-resource "czar" to help ascertain the casualties produced by the multitude of programs affecting youth? In the absence of accurate information, public policy will continue to fall short of the mark. One wonders how a juvenile judge would react to a computer printout that exhibits cost factors, length of institution stay, and type of services for all the youth that pass through his chambers in a given period of time. (How would he respond to seeing a youth incarcerated for seven years on an original delinquent act of runaway?)

This brings us to another important point. A computerized information system is only as reliable and valid—for decision-making—as the processors make it. "Before we process more data we should make sure that what we now process is reasonably 'accurate'."[16] Therefore any attempt at computerizing the juvenile justice system should initially focus on gathering only straightforward information, e.g., data of placement, cost per day, race, age, sex, arrest history by offense. Finally, the objective of computerization of the criminal justice system should be on promoting "equity" of services or punishment, rather than "treatment" cures or "diagnostic impressions." The latter is open to multi-interpretation and unproven remedies and thereby poses a potential "harm effect" equivalent or worse than manual systems. Again, we stress: as discretionary authority is reduced in corrections, e.g., statutory sentencing, many present abuses associated with agencies that use either manual or computerized information systems will disappear.

Finally, to those concerned about data security and agency abuse of confidential information, stringent laws will offset this threat. Considerable violation of confidentiality existed before the introduction of data banks. The current overreaction by agencies to computerization of client files and management-information systems stems more from their fear of exposing program failure and incompetence than protecting clients' rights to privacy. Juvenile justice administrators must learn to appreciate the benefits of accelerating the matching of community resources with individual clients' needs. Thousands of youngsters awaiting community placement are now subjected to endless days in detention centers or relegated to "correctional limbo."[17] If accurate placement information was stored on magnetic tapes and made immediately available to decision-makers, the human suffering associated with such delays would be significantly reduced. Denying children in trouble the advantages of computer technology and evaluation research is tantamount to doctors suppressing life-saving information or ignoring medical advances in the treatment of patients.[18]

7. Adoption of the right to trial by jury for the juvenile offender.

Next to adopting a "flat" sentence for juveniles convicted for a serious offense, the most needed and far-reaching change in juvenile justice would be the provision of a jury trial for the accused. Opponents will argue that this proposal is administratively impractical, inhumane, or inappropriate for "juveniles." I will first address the administrative issue.

Providing a jury trial for individuals accused of serious crimes—in which a guilty verdict may result in long-term imprisonment—is a fundamental right for adults. We know that many if not most indicted adults resort to plea bargaining in the hope of receiving a shorter sentence or probation. In light of limited resources, this trend will more than likely continue for adults and appear for juveniles. Administratively, there is nothing to preclude organizing a jury, made up of three to six members, one of whom will be a youth 14 to 17 years of age. There may be constitutional limitations to expanding jury membership to minors. Pending removal of legal barriers, youth could be appointed in an advisory capacity. A jury trial for juveniles will require minimal coordination effort, additional court personnel, and funds to compensate jury members. Moreover, the policy will promote a greater social investment by young people and the community in the rule of law, and the "justice" process.

In regard to age, it should not be seen as a handicap to receiving due process. When we consider that a young person may be incarcerated for most of his developing years, procedural protection at the entry level cannot be overstated. Admittedly a 7-year-old charged with assault with a deadly weapon may not comprehend the significance of this act, its personal consequences, the advantage of legal representation, or the implications of a trial. However, the child's parents, interested relatives, and an astute public defender should.

A trial by jury will also be viewed by many as cumbersome and antihumanitarian. This suggests that the present juvenile justice process is "streamlined" and "humanitarian." All evidence points to the contrary. Surely, introducing the right of jury trial for juveniles faced with possible incarceration will raise the stature of many juvenile courts and open the juvenile justice process to the public. In this respect, we may speculate that, in the early phase, juries will be inclined to convict the juvenile. This is the result of jury members reacting negatively to what they see as the defendant's rejection of the "paternalistic" and "rehabilitation" model ("tell me the truth and we will help you . . . and if you don't, you must be guilty!"). This observation is supported in research findings, which show that training-school commitments are associated with legal representation.[19] That is, youths who waived their right to counsel in a traditional juvenile court received a more lenient sentence from the court than those who retained counsel. However, upon institutionalization of the jury system this overly punitive reaction will dissipate.

8. Establishment of a juvenile justice commission.

Each state should establish a bipartisan Juvenile Justice Commission. A full-time working organization, membership should be representative of professionals, laymen, and exoffenders. Its program planning and review function should be analogous to the role of a college board of trustees. The commission or board will appoint an administrator to direct the state's juvenile correctional operations. Like a college president, he will be responsible to the commission, while the latter is accountable to the governor. Finally, this body will advise the legislature, the court, and the public on the status of juvenile programs.

9. Adoption of a "risk" education placement formula.

A quarter of the nation's training-school population consists of youth with a home or school problem. These problems have driven them to the streets. It is imperative that we find an alternative—to training schools—in the community. First we must recognize that, in terms of services and resources, these youngsters are and will continue to be in direct competition with thousands of "dependent" and "neglected" youth supervised by private and public child-welfare agencies. The "creaming" and "child-welfare effect," if not controlled, will assure that the "healthiest" and most socially attractive group of youth will be channeled to the most expensive and humane residential settings and foster homes. Young people with the more serious behavior problems will be ignored by these agencies and eventually picked up by the correctional system. A new child-placement policy is demanded.

Financial incentive should be significantly raised to encourage private citizens to take "problem" children into their homes. Because this group is perceived as a high-risk category (more difficult to supervise), payment should be substantially higher to these substitute parents than those who supervise less-difficult youth. Another important factor to be considered by policy-makers is the quality of substitute parenting purchased by public funds.

This investigator believes that individuals with a college background will be more sympathetic toward youth with psychological problems related to parental indifference or rejection than lesser-educated groups. This position means rejecting the "altruistic" philosophy so prevalent in the child-welfare system. (Good foster parents aren't attracted to the money.) It also assaults the "paraprofessionalism" movement. (All this professional education doesn't really mean anything when it comes to "helping" people!!)

Policy makers and professionals who promote low foster-care rates and paraprofessionalism are the last to utilize it or recommend it to friends. They, like most of us, believe that we live in a market economy, where "you get what you pay for." How many parents—with money—willingly send their children with health problems to a paramedic? If a child has a reading problem, is it likely that a middle-class parent will send him to a friendly neighbor—because he has good intentions—to teach him reading? Parents who can afford high standards for their children, be it health care, education, or safe streets, seldom opt for less.

In principle, paraprofessionalism can and should work. What has happened to destroy its credibility is its being used to destroy professionalism and corresponding standards. For example, in the last five years, public welfare agencies have replaced college-trained eligibility workers with high school educated personnel. The result is less money for the poor. (It takes a person with college skills to demystify the welfare regulations!) We observe the highest degree of abuse of paraprofessionalism in the correctional system. Guards, youth leaders, and untrained counselors have literally displaced or driven out professionals. What may have started out as a sincere effort by professionals to open the ranks of human services to people interested in learning "helping skills" has been transformed into a vehicle to provide "cheap labor" to public agencies responsible for services to the most disadvantaged groups. In the long view, the development assures that minority and disadvantaged groups will suffer increased oppression by incompetent and self-serving bureaucrats.

In our society, it has long been accepted that education is not the sole criterion for success. At the same time, education is seen as an attribute and a positive foundation for expanding one's knowledge base. In Camp Kilpatrick, where the entry level for 95 percent of the personnel and all counselors is a B.A. degree, we found staff (unionized and nonunionized) receptive to learning more humanized and professional methods of working with acting-out youngsters. Quite the opposite has been apparent in institutions dominated by personnel with a high school level of education. This group has effectively used collective bargaining and political pressure to resist and defeat program reform.[20]

Offering financial incentive to foster parents to accept high-risk youngsters in their homes will be less difficult to sell as a program than scaling care payment to their education level. The former has been policy in some jurisdictions. Since the late 1960's, the Los Angeles Department of Public Social Services has given supervisors the discretion to pay foster parents of "neglected" and "abused" children a higher child-care rate than provided for the "dependent" AFDC child. Also it is not uncommon for assertive social workers of abused and neglected youth to circumvent inflexible child welfare regulations by incorporating the placement plan in the court report. This strategy results in the court compelling the agency to expend funds in the community it would otherwise spend on the same child if he or she is institutionalized.[21]

A policy of favoring college graduates to work with problem children over less formally educated groups may clash with misguided egalitarians and those who maintain that parenting is an instinct and that "good" parenting is universal. It also threatens the supporters of "cheap" labor who desire to organize larger constituencies for political advantage—extraneous to the needs of displaced youth or the community. This investigator feels that these youngsters deserve substitute parents with the same skills and competences expected in the private sector dealing with the production of goods and services. Corporations continue to prefer college graduates as well as scale salaries and wages to the "risk" of the job. Finally this formula would allow for a special incentive to nondegreed individuals. They will be encouraged to participate in ongoing training in counseling and child care. All participants, regardless of educational attainment, will be required to enroll in an orientation program. They will be instructed in communication skills and supportive techniques found effective in helping aggressive, acting-out, or withdrawn youth. Additional aid will be given to substitute parents who work with youth for an extended period of time. We may even consider a "common-law adoption option" whereby, after a significant time lapse (2-3 years) between parent and child contact—and agreeable to the child and substitute parent—the court approves an adoption grant. Under this arrangement, the adoptive parent(s) and youngster(s) would be eligible for the existing rate of monthly social security survivor's benefits times the "risk" factor. This grant would be less than that distributed to foster parents but not greater than allowed to relatives.

Whatever the extent and the nature of the incentives, the

purpose of this formula is to effect a major policy shift, in which America's thousands of dependent delinquent and non-delinquent youngsters will no longer be exiled to remote, barren, and dehumanizing institutions.

This means that there will be no provision against giving relatives financial incentive to raise children who have lost their parents due to death or neglect. They would receive the same benefits as those provided to common-law adoptive parents. In cases in which relatives are on low, fixed incomes, or pensions, special allowances will be made. Critics will argue that this category should receive significantly less or no financial aid because they are "relatives." This attitude results in trading a child's "roots" for "strangers" or encourages family disintegration. The absurdity of this policy was recently seen in New York City. In March 1975, a "penniless' grandmother, who felt that she could not provide a decent home for her grandson, sent him to Boys Town in Nebraska: "I didn't have no choice. I had no money or nothing—when you have no money, you can't do nothing. They left the kid to me and I haven't heard from them."[22] (Many state regulations prohibit paying foster-care rates to relatives.) The reaction of a Boys Town representative to the above incident was: "It's better than being in the slums of New York City."[23] But how many "poor" youngsters living with relatives are willing to exchange "roots" for a place in an institution? For the money it will cost to institutionalize the 14-year-old boy in question ($10,000-12,000 per year), both he and his grandmother could comfortably move out of the "slum." With half of this income they may be able to survive in most cities.

In summary, more people should be encouraged to become substitute parents of youngsters who, for all practical purposes, fall in the category of "social orphans." Today we have a situation in which many talented citizens including college graduates are unemployed or otherwise engaged in meaningless work. Meanwhile, in the absence of an interested adult and rational social policy, youngsters are permitted to atrophy in remote rural warehouses designed to hold juvenile criminals.

This is not to suggest that appropriate incentives should not be offered to citizens to take "delinquents" in need of a family into their homes. The "risk/education" formula will still apply. But presently, the priority should be on deinstitutionalizing status and minor offenders from "punishment" settings. Such a strategy will also release institutional resources to cope with working with the "violent" juvenile offender. What must be clearly understood is the serious negative social consequences of present child welfare, and delinquency-control policies. In outcome, the present formula produces a "high" dollar cost in "mismatched" services and its equivalent in human casualties.

Two Directions

In conclusion, this investigation has attempted to demystify the therapeutic state and offer viable alternatives to juvenile injustice and rising crime. In the future, if the philosophy of counterdeterrence is not rejected, we may anticipate that the least-serious offenders will continue to be disproportionately subject to coercive "treatment" and incarceration. At the same time, older and more dangerous offenders, benefitting from the "child-welfare effect," will experience shorter sentences or less punishment than may be warranted by the gravity of their crimes. On the other hand, if we opt to establish a rational sentencing structure and noncoercive rehabilitation programs for the juvenile offender—a system that is free of the myths and related negative social consequences of counter deterrence—we will have nothing to lose but juvenile injustice, disrespect of the law and our professional sacred cows.

EPILOGUE:

Officials Respond

This section will present juvenile correctional officials' comments on the indeterminate sentence and decriminalization of status offenders. These observations appeared in the "comment" section of the follow-up survey on institutional stay. Each participant was sent a summary of the national analysis and asked his or her view of the adoption of a fixed sentence and removal of status offenders from the juvenile court. These results appeared in Chapter 6. The following paragraphs are direct quotes from the follow-up questionnaire addressed to the author.

Alabama

All of our commitments are for an indeterminate period of time. Our age range is 12 to 15 years old. We have a Behavior Modification Program using Token Economy for every boy in the Institution. A boy must earn a minimum number of tokens in order to be considered for release. He can earn minimum tokens for release in approximately 7 months. My concern about the modified (fixed) sentence is that it does not allow enough flexibility and approximates too closely the way adult offenders are adjudicated.

Arkansas

Reason(s) for Commitment to Juvenile Services is not stated in the Court Order. The Order only states that the person is a PROPER PERSON FOR COMMITMENT. Factors

143

other than reasons for commitment determine the length of stay in the Training Schools in Arkansas.

California

At this time there is a good deal of conflict between staff and the paroling board regarding these matters. Stated policy and actual practice are often inconsistent. The law is variously interpreted.

Colorado

Thorough initial diagnosis takes into account offenses, circumstances, strengths, and weaknesses of client. The effect of institutionalization has a differential affect on people and their rate of behavior change varies. A system of sentencing by offense is in my opinion rolling Juvenile Correction back in time and focusing on injustice rather than justice. Youth should be released on the basis of professional decisions of growth, change, and community safety.

. . . There should be minimum and maximum on all juvenile commitments.

Connecticut

This data not available since children are not classified by "one-crime" category; most have multiple offenses or problems indicated. Children are committed to this Department for 2 years and spend this time in a variety of residential situations (institution and community), depending on individual treatment program. Some children (direct placements in community) bypass the institution completely. Because of the variety of routes different children travel through their 2-year commitment period, "average stay" is not considered especially useful.

Washington, D.C.

Our court appears to be experimenting with modified fixed sentencing and the training school has no input into this process. The court is requesting progress reports from the training school anywhere from a month after commitment up to a year. At this point we are not too favorably impressed with this trend in fixed sentencing.

Florida

. . . is a juvenile institution designed for problem delinquents from other programs and young people committed for very serious offenses. The answers to the questions above may be very misleading as the majority of the students in our program have spent time in other programs before their transfer. Additionally, approximately one-third of the students in our program are "serious offenders" and may be transfers from the adult system with fixed maximum sentences. Our students tend to remain on parole longer than the average student furloughed from an institution in Florida due to their backgrounds.

. . . is a state-funded treatment program established for adjudicated delinquent boys, ages 14-17. The program is an open, nonsecure living situation where responsible decision-making is stressed. The treatment techniques used are daily Reality Group Therapy meeting and one-to-one counseling. Since our program is not involved in a fixed sentence for our residents, a lot of the questions do not apply.

Iowa

It is difficult to determine exact offense child is committed under. Iowa judges may not specify an offense in court order, only a finding of delinquency.

Kentucky

Each case must be evaluated on its own merits in relation to the decision on the treatment modality to be used and the length of the course of treatment. This would include mitigating factors, the personality behavioral patterns and history of the child, environmental factors in the child's life, whether the child is mentally retarded and the extent of retardation, and neurological or psychiatric conditions. Kentucky uses a modified fixed sentence up to six months which is subject to the prior approval of the Director of Field Services of our Department and which is subject to revision or being set aside by mutual consent of our Department and the committing court. Our Department developed this procedure in order to reduce the number of children who are transferred from Juvenile Court to Circuit Court and to keep children out of the adult correctional system which is not equipped or staffed to provide the type of care and treatment which they require. The Juvenile Court record can be expunged. The Circuit record is permanent.

(Removing status offenders from the juvenile correctional system) was done by the 1972 session of the Kentucky General Assembly and reported out as SB 171 to revise KRS 208.430.* Our agency's handling of that change also enclosed. We have one institution which is used as a last resort exclusively for the treatment of status offenders who cannot be ignored (such as chronic runaways) and with whom all avenues of community treatment have been tried and failed.

---

*Section 1. Section 208.430 of the Kentucky Revised Statutes is amended to read as follows:

(1) Any child committed to the department may on the recommendation of the child welfare worker, at any time during the period of his commitment be:

(a) Discharged from commitment, unless he was committed by a circuit court upon a felony conviction and was given a sentence the period of which will extend beyond the age of twenty-one;

(b) Placed in the home of his parents, or in a suitable foster home, family home, or boarding home, upon such conditions as the department may prescribe and subject to visitation and supervision by a child welfare worker;

(c) Placed in one of the institutions operated by the department; except that no child committed to the department (as a needy, neglected or dependent child), under provision of KRS 208.020 (1) (b), (c), or (d) nor any child 10 years of age or under shall be placed in an institution operated by the department for children committed to the department as delinquents;

(d) Placed in a child-caring institution operated by a local governmental unit or by a private organization willing to receive the child, upon such conditions as the department may prescribe;

(e) Disposed of as provided in KRS 208.460 or 208.470.

(2) Unless the child has been discharged from commitment, any disposition of a child made under this section may at any time during the period of his commitment be changed and other disposition made in accordance with the provisions of this section.

SB 171 amends KRS 430 to prohibit the placement of committed children under ten and children for status crimes (curfew violations, beyond parental control, truancy, etc.) in institutions operated for *delinquents*. This amended statute, which becomes effective June 17, 1972, allows children to be committed to the Department under the above categories but restricts their placement in *delinquent* institutions. SB 171 then will drastically change the direction of Community Services within the Department of Child Welfare. The focus will now be primarily on working with the child committed for status offenses or the child under ten in his own home and community. The following is a list of suggested sequential steps to be followed in working with children coming under the categories of SB 171:

A. Purchase of Care from licensed Private Child-Caring Facility
B. Department of Mental Health Institutions
C. Kentucky Children's Home
D. DCW facilities for youth committed under the categories stipulated by SB 171.

I. The foremost objective is to work with the child in his own home. The following is a list of resources which may be available to the worker to assist him in maintaining the child in his home:

A. Probation with either a court worker, child welfare worker, or volunteer having the responsibility for the child
B. Commitment to the Department (but remaining in his home)
C. Homemaker Services
D. Day Care Services
E. Vocational Rehabilitation
F. Comprehensive Care Centers
G. Day Treatment Facilities
H. Alternate Schools
I. Neighborhood Youth Corps
J. Big Brother/Big Sister Organizations
K. Other public or private social service agencies
L. Boys Clubs

The above list of community resources will not apply completely to all.

II. If it is determined that the child *absolutely* cannot remain in his own home, the next step would be to attempt a regional or area placement. Resources other than the above mentioned community resources which may be utilized for regional or area placements are:

    A. Foster care (regular or hard-to-place)
    B. Vocational schools (residential)
    C. Group homes
    D. Relatives
    E. Halfway houses
    F. YMCA-YWCA
    G. Job Corps
    H. Military
    I. Independent living arrangements (over age 16)
    J. Area resource home (Emergency Shelter Care)

III. If it is determined that the child cannot remain in his own home and a regional or area placement cannot be worked out, the next step would be a statewide placement. All of the community resources listed above would be applicable to a statewide placement.

IV. If all *available* resources have been exhausted for the child in his own home, in a regional or area placement, or in a statewide placement, the next step would be to be referred to an institution. It must be stressed that all available resources—community, regional, area, and statewide—must be exhausted before this referral. The following is a possible institutional resource:

Area Resource Home is an emergency shelter-care facility to be utilized for the placement of youths that are committed to the Department of Child Welfare but cannot be committed to a delinquent institution. This resource home is for temporary placement until more permanent plans are made and will have a maximum limit of 30 days. Each home will also have a maximum capacity of four children. There will be a basic monthly rate for each child placed in the home. A Juvenile Service Worker will be assigned to each home and will be responsible for placement in the home.

As a resource for placement in our institutional program, facilities (IV. D. page 2) for both boys and girls have been established. Naturally this type of placement is to be limited and is to be used

after it has been determined that all resources on the community level
have been thoroughly evaluated [italics added].
. . . I do not feel that the probationary period should be fixed
but should be extended according to need of the individual
under supervision.

Michigan

In the State of Michigan youth who are adjudicated as delinquent become temporary wards of the state under the supervision of the Department of Social Services until they attain
their nineteenth birthday or are discharged by the Department. Every effort is made to provide all youth with services
in the community and only when such efforts fail are youth
placed in an institution. The placement of status-offender-type
youth in institutions is minimal and where it does occur it is
because a workable placement could not be found in the community.

At present, we neither have nor would we support a
modified fixed sentence for our youth.
. . . Please note that although Michigan has a Youth Parole and
Review Board, it is typical here that the Board considers release only after the institution staff has determined readiness.
There are a few occasions where a release is recommended
based on a mandatory annual case review by the Board. Their
N is small, however. In reference to your study findings, I
would surmise that where no offense is reported, it is nonethe-
less known by staff and is a salient factor in staff's view of
readiness for release. Length of institutional stay is often determined in part by the availability of suitable placement resources capable of helping to maintain the youth in the community. In reference to the five states reporting length of stay
by offense, I would suggest that because status offenders tend to
be younger and difficult to place, they may remain in institutions longer than desirable when the relative magnitude of
their violations is considered against the seriousness of Index
crimes. If this is so, a case can be made for improved community placement resources as a prerequisite to eliminating insti-

tutional placement for status offenders. It would be easy for your study to overlook the fact that proper placement is as much a "need" as appropriate treatment in that it establishes a context in which treatment can occur. We no longer receive youth on status offenses only. While I cannot ascertain significance, please note that the five states reporting by offense show a 3.2-month longer stay for those offenders committing crimes against persons as opposed to those showing property offenses. This may raise some question about the study conclusion that the rehabilitation needs of violence-prone youth may be ignored. Also, there may be a study assumption that longer stay implies better recognition of treatment needs. Perhaps so, but the study does not appear to investigate "treatment" as a separate subject.

In reference to . . . "parole" as such . . . our releases are given "conditional releases." That is, they are released from the institution to community supervision and may be revoked if they violate specific special conditions of the release or engage in further delinquencies that result in revocation request from the Community Worker. The policy of the Youth Parole and Review Board is to consider discharge from wardship after at least six months of satisfactory community adjustment. We do not have figures showing average time on release status terminating at discharge.

Missouri

Because the youngsters going through our program are responsible for their own progress, a fixed sentence would negate the positive effects we are having. It has been proven that in the more aggressive offenses or areas where a girl's self-worth is minimal, her stay is longer. (She takes a longer period of time to get through the program to get her head together.)

Montana

Statistics clearly indicate that the recidivism rates (success rates) for juveniles is much higher than for adults. I have always felt that one of the reasons for this was that juveniles could be released when it was felt best for the individual child whereas adults had to serve a definite sentence. Therefore, it seems to me that we are moving in the wrong direction when we start to consider having fixed sentences for juveniles. Likewise I feel very strongly that our desire to treat juveniles like adults has not resulted in more and better services to the juveniles. Since most of the laws are passed by attorneys it appears that recent legislation has been much more successful in increasing the employment rate of attorneys than decreasing crime.

Nebraska

I believe the only offense for which a child should be committed to a juvenile institution should be for juvenile delinquency. If the crime is not serious enough to be called delinquency or if it is too serious to be called delinquency, then he or she should not be in a juvenile institution.

Nevada

I disagree completely with a fixed sentence for juveniles. This is a backward step, in fact would set us back 50 years. We have a treatment plan with certain goals and objectives and while we would experiment with a fixed sentence, I have to see some proof that it is effective. I feel that when the girl or boy accomplishes the objectives the treatment team developed, then even furlough before parole is more effective than determinate sentences.

New York

Professionally feel that safeguard should be instituted to protect "over-incarceration" but sentencing gives rise to "doing time" with little effort extended to effect change or improve.

North Carolina

Rather than parole, we use the term *conditional release*. This service is completely separate from adult parole supervision services. After a child has been on conditional release for approximately one year, he or she is given a satisfactory discharge. However, the committing agency may request and receive a discharge at "any time."

Pennsylvania

One factor I see missing in your report is that society at large has not provided for the emotionally disturbed adolescent. Our view is that the crime, be it drug abuse or auto theft, is the symptom. Over the past five years, the youth that have been committed to our care have changed. We have gone from the classical definition of "delinquent," to the drug user, and now to the emotionally disturbed. We have tried to meet these changes by setting up a therapeutic community within an institution. However, our problem comes from the fact we are ahead of the bureaucratic system, the very one we work for.

South Dakota

Regarding the status offenders, although we do not believe he or she should be committed, our state at the present time does not have the facilities or means to provide help for this type of youngster; this is especially true in the rural and outlying areas of the state.

. . . Our institution is not a lock-up type and therefore I don't feel that we are "abusing" the rights of the juveniles. All of our commitments are discharged when released from the Camp. Only in very rare instances do they go under direct supervision of the Courts.

Tennessee

Status offenders (in my opinion) should not be institutionalized. They appear to pick up a negative antisocial education from their incarceration. We are attempting to get to the real meaning of treatment as opposed to containment. Our students work toward attitudinal changes—which determines their release—we do have minimal commitment stays (3 months for a first offender; 8 months for a repeater).

Utah

Very few youngsters now being committed to this institution (except for short-term observation and diagnosis—60 to 90 days) are for status offenses only. Most status offenders committed—youngsters who have no serious record of law violation—are girls who have failed to respond to any kind of alternatives. A number have been in foster homes, group homes, and in the Youth Center at the State Hospital before commitment to this institution. Typically these youngsters are truants, runaways, suspect or sometimes admitted to being promiscuous, involved in drug use, and failed to respond to any reasonable limits. Example: One girl who has run the full gamut of alternatives ended up in a motel with an older man in Indiana 1500 miles away from home.

This group frequently have had a number of school failures, and are several years behind their grade level in school because apparently there is insufficient structure to insure their remaining in their placement and attending school regularly.

I see many advantages and few disadvantages to the indeterminate commitment in a juvenile institution program such as ours. I think much would depend upon the professional character of the staff and how decisions for release from the institution are made.

With indeterminate commitment, emphasis is placed upon treatment and training, and certain stated goals can be set for each child according to his individual needs. When these goals are reached, he is considered for placement. With a set sentence, I fail to see how many of these goals can be achieved. Safeguards are set up for all cases, including the status offender for periodic administrative reviews to see that youngsters with lesser offenses are not lost in the program and continue for an unreasonable length of time. Most youngsters are seriously academically retarded and we believe that rehabilitation, which frequently means either preparation for employment or continuation of schooling outside the institution, depends upon a makeup of essential classes.

Release is determined by an evaluation and progress of the

youngster, and particularly a measurement against agreed-upon goals which involves a definite program understood by the youngster, and he knows that release is contingent upon meeting the agreed-upon goals. His behavior is tracked continually by use of computer and he is informed weekly of his progress.

I can see no system that is better than this if properly administered. Such a program depends upon an adequate staff of qualified clinicians and an educational program capable of delivering the needed educational services. We believe we have both.

Vermont

Under new legislation this year [1974] the status offenders referred to the state agency goes through an additional step—referring agency must show court that all other available alternatives were reviewed before considering placement. Also upon admission, evaluation staff must state not only the problems but treatment strategies to be used and probable length of stay with a 30-day review.

West Virginia

We have peer groups who decide when a student should be released.

Wisconsin

Wisconsin statute defines agencies' responsibility with respect to so-called status offender—as "person in need of supervision"—who may be supervised but not institutionalized as such.

Passage of Wisconsin's 18-year-majority law in 1972 drastically altered previous experience. Child must be released from supervision at age 18 without regard to his readiness on capability to assume responsibility.

APPENDIX

CHAPTER 2

Table A

SUMMARY TABLE:
THREE-WAY ANALYSIS OF VARIANCE ON STAY

Source	SS	df	Var. Est.	f	Sign.
Institution Size[a] (rows)	19.92	1	19.92	1.48	NS[d]
Classification[b] (blocks)	63.01	1	63.01	4.86	<.05
Release Mode[c] (columns)	.30	1	.30	.02	NS
R x B	10.87	1	10.87	.84	NS
R x C	25.42	1	25.42	1.96	NS
B x C	40.41	1	40.41	3.12	NS
R x B x C	22.01	1	22.01	1.70	NS
Within	1361.78	105	12.97		
TOTAL	1543.72	112	13.78		

[a]Small—less than 100 residents, Large—100 or more residents
[b]I Level/Quay, APA or other
[c]Parole Board, No Parole Board
[d]Not statistically significant

CHAPTER 3

Table A

1972 THREE MONTH COHORT—686 CASES
SUMMARY OF SIGN. ANALYSIS OF VARIANCE OF
STAY AVERAGE TOTAL INSTITUTIONAL STAY

Race	N	Mean	Std. Dev.	T-Test	Sign.
"A" Insti Females					
White	93	211 (days)	94		
				1.99	<.02
Black	39	246	91		
Institution					
A	132	221	94		
				9.8	<.001
B	17	422	77		
Return Status					
Males					
Returned	133	226	138		
				2.8	<.01
Discharged	219	189	75		
White					
Returned	87	228	155		
				2.00	<.02
Discharged	127	192	74		
Black					
Returned	46	223	99		
				2.20	<.02
Discharged	92	186	76		

Category	D.F.	Mean Sq.	F	Sign.
Institution Males				
Age Between	31	110366		
			13.26	<.01
Within	496	8325		
Race Between	15	212801		
			25.0	<.01
Within	512	8513		
Off Between	31	106912		
			12.50	<.01
Within	494	8552		
Male Between	7	437822		
Insti			50.75	<.001
Within	520	8626		

Table B

RELATIONSHIP BETWEEN STATE X's AVERAGE LENGTH OF STAY IN
"RELEASING INSTITUTION"[a] AND OFFENSE AT COMMITMENT BY RACE, INSTITUTION
AND ORGANIZATION ORIENTATION—1974 COHORT

Offense Category	Releasing Institution and Orientation								
	CUSTODY								
	"A"-Female (N=133)		"A"-Male (N=320)		"C"-Male (N=30)				
	White	Black	White	Black	White	Black			
I Index Against Person	157 (days)	269	144	155	—[b]	297			
II Index Against Property	67	129	149	155	141	281			
III Other Felonies & Misd.	159	206	164	163	210	210			
IV Status & Minor Misd.	178	197	149	182	220	247			
	TREATMENT								
	"B"-Female (N=17)		"B"-Male (N=17)		"D"-Male (N=15)				
	White	Black	White	Black	White	Black			
I Index Against Person	317	329	—	352	432	—			
II Index Against Property	405	353	370	355	435	362			
III Other Felonies & Misd.	435	304	349	—	377	367			
IV Status & Minor Misd.	388	—	525	—	317	471			

[a]Excludes stay in diagnostic or other institutions or camps; excludes cases assigned to camps
[b]No cases fell in this category

Table C

FREQUENCY DISTRIBUTION BY PERCENT
OF AVERAGE TOTAL INSTITUTIONAL
STAY BY RACE AND SEX—523 CASES

Interval	Female		Male	
	White	Black	White	Black
0-99 days	2%	0%	5%	2%
100-199	41	32	54	60
200-299	42	44	22	22
300-399	6	14	9	7
400-499	4	5	5	6
500 and over	5	5	5	3
Total	100%	100%	100%	100%

Table D

RELATIONSHIP BETWEEN AVERAGE TOTAL
QUARTILE INSTITUTIONAL STAY AND
RETURN RATE—353 MALES

Institution Stay	Percent Returned
First Quartile (0-154 days)	36 percent
Second Quartile (155-188 days)	27
Third Quartile (189-270 days)	39
Fourth Quartile (271 days and over)	32

CHAPTER 5

Table A

ONE-WAY ANALYSIS OF VARIANCE OF
RELATIONSHIP BETWEEN AGE AND AVERAGE
LENGTH OF PAROLE BY SEX

Source	D.F.	Sum of Squares	Mean Squares	F Ratio	Sign
(Females—118 Cases)					
Between Groups	3	315216	105072	7.88	< .01
Within Groups	114	1519819	13331		
Total	117	1835035			
(Males—387 Cases)					
Between Groups	3	1502752	500919	22.28	< .01
Within Groups	383	8610064	22480		
Total	386	10112816			

Table B

AVERAGE DAYS ON PAROLE BY AGE
CATEGORY AND SEX—405 CASES

	10-14 years		15 years		16 years		17 years and older	
	Male	Female	Male	Female	Male	Female	Male	Female
Mean	371	370	365	355	339	339	229	243
Std. Dev.	174	91	138	127	160	128	141	99
N	48	11	83	35	104	32	152	40

Table C

PERCENT OF MALES RETURNED
BY AGE CATEGORY AND RACE—131 CASES

Age at Commitment	Race	
	Black	White
10-14 years	24 percent	27
15 years	41	34
16 years	26	30
17 and over	9	9
Total	100	100

Table D

PERCENT OF TOTAL MALE ADMISSION
POPULATION (1972 COHORT) COMPARED TO
RETURN RATE BY AGE—528 CASES

Age	Percent of Adm. Population	Percent Returned
10-14 years	16%	26%
15 years	25	37
16 years	27	28
17 and over	32	9
Total	100%	100%

Table E

FREQUENCY DISTRIBUTION BY PERCENT OF
AVERAGE DAYS OF PAROLE BY
RACE AND SEX—481 CASES[a]

Interval	Female		Male	
	White	Black	White	Black
0-99 days	3%	0%	12%	7%
100-199	24	16	24	18
200-299	18	31	19	20
300-399	25	21	16	20
400-499	24	24	15	16
500 and over	6	8	14	19
Total	100%	100%	100%	100%

[a]Excludes cases returned or recommitted

NOTES

Prologue
1. Nicholas N. Kittrie, *The Right to be Different* (Baltimore: Pelican Books Inc., 1973) pp. 10-40.
2. *Ibid.*, p. 27.
3. *Ibid.*, p. 3.
4. *Ibid.*, pp. 46-47.
5. Irving Kristol, "Taxes, Poverty and Equality," *The Public Interest*, No. 37, (Fall) 1974, pp. 3-29.
6. *Ibid.*, p. 21.

1 Youth and Crime: The Social Consequences of Counterdeterrence
1. *U.S. Bureau of the Census, Statistical Abstract of the United States 1973* (Washington, D.C.: U.S. Government Printing Office, 1973) p. 151.
2. *Uniform Crime Report 1972* (Washington, D.C.: U.S. Government Printing Office, 1973) pp. 37, 122.
3. *Uniform Crime Report 1973* (Washington, D.C.: U.S. Government Printing Office, 1974) p. 17.
4. *Ibid.*, p. 22.
5. *Ibid.*, p. 13.
6. *Ohio Youth Commission Statistical Report, 1973.*
7. *Statistical Abstract, op. cit.*
8. *Juvenile Delinquency in Illinois, Highlights of the 1972 Adolescent Survey* (Chicago: Institute for Juvenile Research, Department of Mental Health, State of Illinois, 1972).
9. *Ibid.*, pp. 17-26.
10. *Ibid.*, p. 10.

11. *Ibid.*, p. 11.
12. Norval Morris and Gordon Hawkins, *The Honest Politician's Guide to Crime Control* (Chicago: University of Chicago Press, 1970), p. 157.
13. *Ibid.*
14. *Task Force Report, Juvenile Delinquency and Youth Crime—The President's Commission on Law Enforcement and Administration of Justice 1967* (Washington, D.C.: U.S. Government Printing Office, 1968) p. 19.
15. Frank Zimring, *Perspective on Deterrence* (Washington, D.C.: U.S. Government Printing Office, 1971) p. 3.
16. Peter P. Lejins, "Recent Changes in the Concept of Prevention," Proceedings of the Ninety-fifth Annual Congress of Correction (Reprint), American Correctional Association, 1965, p. 149.
17. *Ibid.*
18. Gordon Tullock, "Does Punishment Deter Crime?" *The Public Interest*, No. 36, Summer 1974.
19. Zimring, *op. cit.*, p. 57.
20. *Uniform Crime Report 1972, op. cit.*, pp. 62-66.
21. Herbert E. Klarman, "Major Public Initiatives in Health Care," *The Public Interest*, No. 34, Winter 1973, p. 118.
22. *Statistical Abstract, op. cit.*, p. 75.

2 The Myth of the Indeterminate Sentence

1. U.S. Bureau of the Census, *Statistical Abstract of the United States, 1973* (Washington, D.C.: U.S. Government Printing Office, 94th Edition, 1973), p. 162.
2. Sol Rubin, "Illusion of Treatment in Sentences and Crime Commitments," *Crime and Delinquency*, Vol. 16, No. 1, January 1970, pp. 70-92; Nigel Walker, *Sentencing in a Rational Society* (New York: Basic Books, Inc., 1971), pp. 113-130; D. A. Thomas, *Principles of Sentencing*, (London: Heinemann Educational Books, Ltd., 1970), pp. 35-45.
3. Walker, *op. cit.*, pp. 113-130.
4. *Ibid.*
5. D. A. Thomas, *op. cit.*, p. 35.

6. *Ibid.,* p. 38.
7. *Ibid.,* p. 244.
8. Shlomo Shoham and Mosh Sandberg, "Suspended Sentences in Israel—An Evaluation of the Preventive Efficacy of Prospective Imprisonment," *Crime & Delinquency,* Vol. 10, No. 1, January 1964, pp. 74-83.
9. Walker, *op. cit.,* p. 72.
10. Sol Rubin, "Long Prison Terms and the Form of Sentence," *NPPA Journal,* Vol. 1, No. 2, April 1956, pp. 337-351.
11. Sol Rubin, "Illusions of Treatment in Sentences and Crime Commitments," *op. cit.*
12. W. Vaughan Stapleton and Lee E. Teitelbaum, *In Defense of Youth* (New York: Russell Sage Foundation, 1972) pp. 11-14.
13. *Ibid.*
14. Lois G. Forer, "A Children and Youth Court: A Modest Proposal," *Legal Rights of Children* (Fair Lawn, New Jersey, R. E. Burdick, Inc., 1973) p. 49; Gerald R. Wheeler and Hervey Inskeep, "Youth in the Gauntlet," *Federal Probation,* December 1968.
15. Stuart King Jeffary, *Sentencing of Adults in Canada* (Toronto: University of Toronto Press, 1963).
16. A. Kahn, "From Delinquency Treatment of Community Development," in S. Lazarsfeld, et al. (ed.), *The Uses of Sociology* (New York: Basic Books, 1967) pp. 477, 480.
17. Rubin, *op. cit.*
18. *Ibid.*
19. Irvin Ben Cooper, *Crime and Delinquency,* Vol. 17, No. 1, January 1961, pp. 9-15.
20. Frank W. Miller, *The Juvenile Justice Process* (Mineola, N.Y., The Foundation Press, Inc., 1971), pp. 1209-1216.
21. *Ibid.*
22. Stephen Wizner, "The Child and State: Adversaries in the Juvenile Justice System," A symposium edited by Columbia Human Rights Law Review (Fair Lawn, N.J., R. E. Burdick, Inc., 1973) pp. 101-111.
23. Walker, *op. cit.,* p. 126.

24. Lamar T. Empey and Steven G. Lubeck, *The Silverlake Experiment* (Chicago: Aldine Publishing Co., 1971) pp. 307-309.
25. *Ibid.*, p. 308.
26. *Ibid.*
27. The Status of Current Research in the California Youth Authority, *Annual Report*, July 1972, Department of the Youth Authority, State of California, 1972, p. 9.
28. David Street, Robert D. Vinter, and Charles Perrow, *Organization for Treatment* (New York: The Free Press, 1966) pp. 196-197.
29. Donnell M. Pappenfort and Dee Morgan Kilpatrick, *A Census of Children's Residential Institutions in the United States, Puerto Rico, and the Virgin Islands: 1966* (Chicago: Social Service Monographs, Second Series, Volume 3, The School of Social Service Administration, The University of Chicago, 1970).
30. *Ibid.*, p. 29.
31. *Statistics on Public Institutions for Delinquent Children, 1970* (Washington, D.C.: U.S. Government Printing Office, Department of Health, Education, and Welfare, 1970) p. 4.

3 A Longitudinal Study of Juvenile Incarceration and Effects of Prisonization

1. See Nigel Walker, *Sentencing in a Rational Society* (New York: Basic Books, 1971) pp. 113-130; D. A. Thomas, *Principles of Sentencing* (London: Heinemann Educational Books, Ltd., 1970) pp. 35-45; Irwin Ben Cooper, *Crime and Delinquency* Vol. 17, No. 1, January, 1961, pp. 9-15; Stuart King Jeffary, *Sentencing of Adults in Canada* (Toronto: University of Toronto Press, 1963).
2. Sol Rubin, "Long Prison Terms and the Form of Sentence," *NPPA Journal*, Vol. 1, No. 2, April 1956, pp. 337-351.
3. *Sentencing Alternatives and Procedures* (American Bar Association, 1967) p. 85.
4. Council of Judges of the National Council on Crime and Delinquency, *Model Sentencing Act Second Edition* (National

Council on Crime and Delinquency [N.C.C.D.] 1972) p. 2.

5. Joseph E. Scott, "The Use of Discretion in Determining the Severity of Punishment for Incarcerated Offenders," *The Journal of Criminal Law and Criminology,* Vol. 65, No. 2, June 1974, pp. 214-224.

6. "Toward a New Corrections Policy," *Crime and Justice,* Vol. 2, The Academy for Contemporary Problems, 1501 Neil Avenue, Columbus, Ohio 42301, p. 8.

7. W. Vaughan Stapleton and Lee E. Teitelbaum, *In Defense of Youth* (New York: Russell Sage Foundation, 1972) pp. 11-14.

8. Donnell M. Pappenfort and Dee Morgan Kilpatrick, *A Census of Children's Residential Institutions in the United States, Puerto Rico, and the Virgin Islands: 1966* (Chicago: Social Service Monographs, Second Series, Vol. 3, The School of Social Service Administration, The University of Chicago, 1970) p. 29.

9. See Donald Clemmer, *The Prison Community* (Boston: Christopher Publishing Company, 1940).

10. See Don M. Gottfredson *et al.,* "Four Thousand Lifetimes: A Study of Time Served and Parole Outcomes." (David: National Council on Crime and Delinquency, 1973) pp. 27-29.

11. Simon Dinitz and Stuart J. Miller, "Measuring Institutional Impact: A Follow-up," *Criminology,* Vol. II, No. 3, November 1973, pp. 417-426.

12. Quoted from Harry E. Allen, "The Indeterminate Sentence in America: An Empirical Test," presented at the Western Division of the American Society of Criminology in San Jose, California, May 3, 1974.

13. Donnell M. Pappenfort, Clifton Rhodes, and Margaret Sebastian, "Factors Accounting for Variation in Use of Public Institutions for Delinquent Children in the United States and in Expenditures for Their Care," A Report of Research carried out under contract with the National Assessment Study of Correctional Programs for Juvenile and Youthful Offenders with support of Grant N 172-014-6 to

the University of Michigan by the U.S. Department of Justice Law Enforcement Assistance Administration.

14. *Ibid.*, p. 19.
15. *Ibid.*, p. 10.
16. *Ibid.*, p. 15; see Pappenfort et al., *Census of Children's Institutions*, Tables 137-159, pp. 140-167.

4 Reflections on the Revolving Door and Institutional Individualization

1. Douglas Jansson, "Developing A State Strategy For Community Based Corrections," (unpublished monograph) Office of Policy Research, State of Ohio, July 12, 1973.
2. See Paul N. Williams, "Boys Town: An Expose Without Bad Guys," *Columbia Journalism Review*, Vol. 13, No. 5, January/February 1975, pp. 30-38.
3. *Ibid.*, p. 33.
4. *Ibid.*, p. 37.
5. *Ibid.*
6. *Ibid.*, p. 35.
7. *Ibid.*, pp. 30-38.
8. *Ibid.*, p. 37.

5 Juvenile Parole: Extending the Therapeutic State

1. Sol Rubin, *The Law of Criminal Correction* (St. Paul: West Publishing Co., 1963), p. 544.
2. G. I. Giardini, *The Parole Process* (Springfield, Ill.: Charles C Thomas, 1959), p. 12.
3. Statistical Abstract of the United States 1973, U.S. Bureau of the Census, U.S. Government Printing Office, 94th Edition, 1973, p. 162.
4. Gerald R. Wheeler, "National Analysis of Institutional Length of Stay: The Myth of the Indeterminate Sentence," *Monograph*, Ohio Youth Commission, 1974.
5. Giardini, *op. cit.*, pp. 5-6.
6. See Vincent O'Leary, "Issues and Trends in Parole Administration in the United States," *The American Criminal Law Review*, Vol. II, No. 1, Fall 1972, p. 101. Joseph E. Scott, "The

Use of Discretion in Determining the Severity of Punishment for Incarcerated Offenders," *The Journal of Criminal Law and Criminology*, Vol. 65, No. 2, June 1974, pp. 214-224.

7. Sol Rubin, "Illusion of Treatment in Sentences and Crime Commitments," *Crime and Delinquency*, Vol. 16, No. 1, January 1970.

8. The degrees of freedom and mean square were (7) and (137211.2) for between variance and (502) and (24237.4) for within variance.

9. See Marvin Wolfgang, Robert M. Figlio, and Thorsten Sellin, *Delinquency in a Birth Cohort* (Chicago: University of Chicago Press, 1972); as quoted from Gene Kassebaum, *Delinquency and Social Policy* (Englewood Cliffs: Prentice Hall, Inc., 1974), p. 113.

6 Attitudes toward a Fixed Sentence for Juvenile Offenders

1. *Juvenile and Adult Correctional Institutions and Agencies Directory 1972*, (College Park, Maryland: The American Correctional Association, 1973).

2. Donnell M. Pappenfort and Dee Morgan Kilpatrick, *A Census of Children's Residential Institutions in the United States, Puerto Rico, and the Virgin Islands: 1966* (Chicago: Social Service Monographs, Second Series, Volume 3, The School of Social Service Administration, The University of Chicago, 1970).

3. Dean Luxford, Letter received from Superintendent, Training School for Girls, Mitchelville, Iowa, April 30, 1974.

4. *Model Sentencing Act, Second Edition* (National Council on Crime and Delinquency, 1972).

7 PINS: Dilemmas of Decriminalization

1. *Task Force Report: Juvenile Delinquency and Youth Crime, The President's Commission on Law Enforcement and Administration of Justice 1967* (Washington, D.C.: U.S. Government Printing Office, 1968) p. 25.

2. Stuart Stiller and Carol Elder, "PINS—A Concept in Need

of Supervision," *The American Criminal Law Review*, Vol. 12, No. 1, Summer 1974, p. 33.

3. *Ibid*, p. 34.
4. *Ibid*.
5. *Ibid*.
6. New York Family Court Act Section 712 (1963).
7. Illinois Juvenile Court Act Section 702-3 (1966).
8. Maryland Annotated Code Section 2-801.
9. District of Columbia Annotated Code Section 16-2320 (1973); California Welfare and Institutions Code Section 602 (1972).
10. Maryland Annotated Code Section 3-823.
11. *Ibid*, Section 3-832.
12. Task Force Report *op.cit.*
13. *Ibid*, pp. 25-35.
14. Stiller and Elder *op.cit.*, p. 36.
15. *Ibid*; see *In re Gault*, 387 U.S. 1, 29 (1967).
16. *In re Winship*, 397 U.S. 358 (1970), as quoted in Stiller and Elder *op.cit.* p. 37.
17. Terence P. Thornberry, "Race, Socioeconomic Status and Sentencing in the Juvenile Justice System," *The Journal of Criminal Law and Criminology* Vol. 64, No. 1, 1973, pp. 90-98.
18. Helen Sumner, "Locking Them Up," *Crime and Delinquency*, Vol. 7, No. 2, April 1971, p. 173.
19. *Ibid*.
20. *The PINS Child, A Plethora of Problems* (New York: Office of Children's Services, November 1973) p. 76.
21. See Annual Statistical Report 1973, Ohio Youth Commission, Columbus, Ohio.
22. Stiller and Elder, *op.cit.*, p. 42.
23. *Ibid*, p. 39.
24. *Ibid*, pp. 42-43.
25. *The PINS Child, A Plethora of Problems*, p. 62.
26. *Ibid*, p. 8.
27. *Ibid*, p. 56.
28. See Gerald R. Wheeler "National Analysis of Institutional

Length of Stay" *Monograph* (Ohio Youth Commission) April 1974.
29. Wheeler, "A New Policy of Juvenile Incarceration" (unpublished manuscript).
30. Maryland Annotated Code Section 3-823 and Section 3-832.

8 The Case for Noncoercive Humanitarianism
1. See Robert Martinson, "What Works?—Questions and Answers about Prison Reform," *The Public Interest*, No. 35 (Spring 1974).
2. Lawrence S. Root, "State Work Release Programs: An Analysis of Operational Policies," *Federal Probation*, Vol. 37, No. 4 (December 1973) p. 56.
3. *Ibid.*
4. Jeff C. Goldsmith, *Youth and the Public Sector* (Chicago, The University of Chicago, The School of Social Service Administration, the Center for the Study of Welfare Policy, Grant No. 10-P-560201 5-02, September 1972) p. B-5; Gerald R. Wheeler, "America's New Street People: Implications for the Human Services," *Social Work*, Vol. 16, No. 3 (July 1971), pp. 19-24.
5. *Columbus Dispatch*, December 17, 1972.
6. See Gerald R. Wheeler, "A Study of Client Characteristics, Egalitarian Orientation and Institutional Factors Related to Response Pattern to Public and Voluntary Free Health Services," (unpublished dissertation) The University of Chicago, The School of Social Service Administration, March, 1974.
7. Quote from Long Beach Free Clinic's Agreement with Los Angeles County Board of Supervisors, September 17, 1969.
8. *Columbus Dispatch*, December 17, 1972.
9. Irving Spergel, *Community Problem Solving: the Delinquency Example* (Chicago: University of Chicago Press, 1969) pp. 31-32.
10. *Ibid.*
11. *Ibid.*

12. Interview with Merry Morash, Ph.D. student, University of Maryland, November 25, 1974, and principal author of the Law Enforcement Assistance Administration's funded Community Arbitration Board Project, Anne Arundel County, Maryland.

9 A New Policy of Juvenile Justice

1. Interview with Kraig Vogt, Director of Children's Services, Fort Mitchell Catholic Children's Home, Fort Mitchell, Kentucky, January 5, 1975.
2. Interview with Lawrence Jamison, Legal Counsel for Prisoners' Rights Association, and Associate Professor, Institute of Criminology, University of Maryland.
3. David Larom, ACSW, Director Anne Arundel County Juvenile Services (Memorandum), August 16, 1973; see Article 26, Sec. 70-88, Annotated Code of Maryland.
4. *Ibid.*
5. *Evening Capital,* August 22, 1973.
6. See California's Welfare Institutions Code, Sec. 600, 601 and 602.
7. The writer gratefully acknowledges the assistance of Merry Morash, Ph.D. student, University of Maryland, Institute of Criminal Justice and Criminology, in gathering material on citation program.
8. *New York Times,* August 7, 1972.
9. See *Time,* September 2, 1974.
10. Marvin E. Frankel, *Criminal Sentences: Law without Order* (New York: Hill & Wang, 1972), p. 5.
11. *Ibid.,* p. 6.
12. See *Washington Post,* February 17, 1975.
13. Leslie T. Wilkins, personal communication.
14. John Dearden and Richard L. Nolan, "How to Control the Computer Resource," *Harvard Business Review,* November-December 1973, pp. 68-69.
15. See Carolyn L. Kenton, "Modern Legislative Staffing," *State Government,* Vol. XLVII, No. 3, Summer 1974.
16. Leslie T. Wilkins, personal communication.

17. See Gerald R. Wheeler and Harvey Inskeep, III, "Youth in the Gauntlet," *Federal Probation*, Vol. 32, No. 4, December 1968, pp. 21-25.
18. See Leslie T. Wilkins, "Directions for Corrections," *American Philosophical Society*, Vol. 118, No. 3, June 1974, pp. 235-247.
19. W. V. Stapleton and L. E. Teitelbaum, *In Defense of Youth* (New York: Russell Sage Foundation, 1972), p. 66.
20. From August 1971 to September 1972, I was Deputy Superintendent, Fairfield School for Boys, Lancaster, Ohio. The second largest training school and the first built (1857), its personnel in charge of "custody" became unionized in the late 1960's. For 12 consecutive months, the new superintendent and myself struggled with union grievances over issues such as abolishing silence in the cottages, abolishing military uniforms and marching, permitting afro haircuts, and abolition of inmate guards, etc., etc. (One of the unique punishments that we attempted to change was called "wall time." In this situation, a youth accused of any infraction was required to stand nose against the wall for every spare minute excepting meals and bedtime for periods up to three weeks.) In literally every (15) cottage, boys were relegated to the basement during activity period. Needless to say, the union threatened strikes and took their case to the state representative and community. Both the Superintendent, Gerald J. Novack, and I were transferred to the central administration.
21. See Gerald R. Wheeler "Children of the Court: A Profile of Poverty," *Crime & Delinquency*, April 1971, pp. 152-159.
22. See *Columbus Dispatch*, March 16, 1975.
23. *Ibid.*

BIBLIOGRAPHY

Allen, Harry E., "The Indeterminate Sentence in America: An Empirical Test," Presented at the Western Division of the American Society of Criminology in San Jose, California, May 3, 1974.

Annual Statistical Report, 1973, Ohio Youth Commission, Columbus, Ohio.

Clemmer, Donald, *The Prison Community* (Boston: Christopher Publishing Company, 1940).

Columbus Dispatch, December 17, 1972.

Columbus Dispatch, March 16, 1975.

Cooper, Irwin Ben, *Crime and Delinquency,* Vol. 17, No. 1, January 1961.

Council of Judges of the National Council on Crime and Delinquency, *Model Sentencing Act Second Edition* (National Council on Crime and Delinquency (N.C.C.D.) 1972).

Dearden, Joan and Richard L. Nolan, "How to Control the Computer Resource," *Harvard Business Review,* November-December 1973.

Dinitz, Simon, and Stuart J. Miller, "Measuring Institutional Impact: A Follow-up," *Criminology,* Vol. II, No. 3, November 1973.

District of Columbia Annotated Code Section 16-2320 (1973); California Welfare and Institution Code Section 602 (1972).

Empey, Lamar T., and Steven A. Lubeck, *The Silverlake Experiment* (Chicago: Aldine Publishing Company, 1971).

Evening Capital, August 22, 1973.

Forer, Lois G., "A Children and Youth Court: A Modest Proposal," *Legal Rights of Children*, (Fair Lawn, New Jersey, R. E. Burdock, Inc., 1973).

Frankel, Marvin E., *Criminal Sentences: Law Without Order* (New York: H. W. & Wang, 1972).

Giardini, G. D. *The Parole Process* (Springfield, Illinois: Charles C Thomas, 1959).

Goldsmith, Jeff C. *Youth and the Public Sector* (Chicago: The University of Chicago, The School of Social Service Administration, the Center for the Study of Welfare Policy, Grant No. 10-P-560201 5-02, September 1972).

Gottfredson, Don M., et.al., "Four Thousand Lifetimes: A Study of Time Service and Parole Outcomes." (Davis, California: National Council on Crime and Delinquency, 1973).

Illinois Juvenile Court Act Section 702-3 (1966).

Jamison, Lawrence, Legal Council for Prisoners' Rights Association and Associate Professor, Institute of Criminology, University of Maryland (Interview).

Jansson, Douglas, "Developing a State Strategy for Community Based Corrections," (unpublished monograph), Office of Policy Research, State of Ohio, July 12, 1973.

Jeffary, Stuart King, *Sentencing of Adults in Canada* (Toronto: University of Toronto Press, 1963).

Juvenile and Adult Correctional Institutions and Agencies Directory 1972, (College Park, Maryland: The American Correctional Association, 1973).

Juvenile Delinquency in Illinois, Highlights of the 1972 Adolescent Survey (Chicago: Institute for Juvenile Research Department of Mental Health, State of Illinois, 1972).

Juvenile Delinquency and Youth Crime: The President's Commission on Law Enforcement and Administration of Justice, 1967 (Washington, D.C. U.S. Government Printing Office, 1968).

Kahn, A. "From Delinquency Treatment of Community Development," in S. Lazarsfeld, et al. (ed.), *The Uses of Sociology* (New York: Basic Books, 1967).

Kassebaum, Gene, *Delinquency and Social Policy* (Englewood Cliffs: Prentice Hall, Inc., 1974).

Kearman, Herbert E. "Major Public Initiation in Health Care," *The Public Interest,* No. 34, Winter 1973.

Kenton, Carolyn L. "Modern Legislation Staffing," *State Government,* Vol. XLVII, No. 3, Summer 1974.

Kittrie, Nicholas N. *The Right to be Different* (Baltimore: Pelican Books Inc., 1973).

Kristol, Irving, "Texas, Poverty, and Equality," *The Public Interest,* No. 37, Fall 1974.

Larom, David, ACSW, Director, Anne Arundel County Juvenile Services (Memorandum), August 16, 1973: see Article 26, Sec. 70-88, Annotated Code of Maryland.

Lejins, Peter P. "Recent Changes in the Concept of Prevention," Proceedings of the Ninety-fifth Annual Congress of Correction (Reprint), American Correctional Association, 1965.

Long Beach Free Clinic's Agreement with Los Angeles County Board of Supervisors, September 17, 1969.

Luxford, Dean. Letter received from Superintendent Training School for Girls, Mitchelville, Iowa, April 30, 1974.

Martinson, Robert, "What Works?—Questions and Answers about Prison Reform," *The Public Interest,* No. 35, Spring 1974.

Maryland Annotated Code Sections 2-801, 3-823 and 3-832.

Miller, Frank W. *The Juvenile Justice Process* (Mineola, N.Y.: The Foundation Press, Inc., 1971).

Morash, Merry, Ph.D. student, University of Maryland, November 25, 1974, and principal author of the Law Enforcement Assistance Administration-funded Community Arbitration Board Project, Anne Arundel County, Maryland.

Morris, Norval and Gordon Hawkins, *The Honest Politician's Guide to Crime Control* (Chicago: University of Chicago Press, 1970).

New York Family Court Act Section 712 (1963).

New York Times, August 7, 1972.

Ohio Youth Commission Statistical Report, 1973.

O'Leary, Vincent. "Issues and Trends in Parole Administration in the United States," *The American Criminal Law Review,* Vol. II, No. 1, Fall 1972.

Pappenfort, Donnell M. and Dee Morgan Kilpatrick, *A Census of Children's Residential Institutions in the United States, Puerto Rico, and the Virgin Islands: 1966*. (Chicago: Social Service Monographs, Second Series, Vol. 3, The School of Social Service Administration, The University of Chicago, 1970).

Pappenfort, Donnell M. and Clifton Rhodes and Margaret Sebastian, "Factors Accounting for Variation in Use of Public Institutions for Delinquent Children in the United States and in Expenditures for their Care," A Report of Research carried out under contract with the National Assessment Study of Correctional Program for Juvenile and Youthful Offenders with support of Grant N-172-014-6 to the University of Michigan by U.S. Department of Justice Law Enforcement Assistance Administration.

The PINS Children, A Plethora of Problems (New York: Office of Children's Services, November 1973).

Root, Lawrence C. "State Work Release Programs: An Analysis of Operational Policies," *Federal Probation*, Vol. 37, No. 4 December 1973.

Rubin, Sol, "Illusion of Treatment in Sentences and Crime Commitments," *Crime and Delinquency*, Vol. 16, No. 1, January 1970.

Rubin, Sol, *The Law of Criminal Correction* (St. Paul: West Publishing Company, 1963).

Rubin, Sol, "Long Prison Terms and the Form of Sentence," *NPPA Journal*, Vol. 1, No. 2, April 1956.

Scott, Joseph E. "The Use of Discretion in Determining the Severity of Punishment for Incarcerated Offenders," *The Journal of Criminal Law and Criminology*, Vol. 65, No. 2, June 1974.

Sentencing Alternatives and Procedures (American Bar Association, 1967).

Shoham, Shlomo, and Mosh Sandberg, "Suspended Sentences in Israel—An Evaluation of the Preventive Efficacy of Prospective Imprisonment," *Crime and Delinquency*, Vol. 10, No. 1, January 1964.

Spergel, Irving, Community Problem: Solving the Delinquency

Example (Chicago: University of Chicago Press, 1969).

Stapleton, W. Vaughn, and Lee E. Teitelbaum, *In Defense of Youth* (New York: Russell Sage Foundation 1972).

Statistical Abstract of the United States 1973, U.S. Bureau of the Census, U.S. Government Printing Office, 94th Edition, 1973.

Statistics on Public Institutions for Delinquent Children, 1970, (Washington, D.C.: U.S. Government Printing Office, Department of Health, Education, and Welfare, 1970).

The Status of Current Research in the California Youth Authority, *Annual Report,* July 1972, Department of the Youth Authority, State of California 1972.

Stiller, Stuart, and Carol Elder. "PINS—A Concept in Need of Supervision," *The American Criminal Law Review,* Vol. 12, No. 1 Summer 1974.

Street, David, Robert D. Vinter, and Charles Perrow, *Organization for Treatment* (New York: The Free Press, 1969).

Sumner, Helen, "Locking Them Up," *Crime and Delinquency,* Vol. 7, No. 2, April 1971.

Thomas, D. A. *Principles of Sentencing* (London: Heinemann Educational Books, Ltd. 1970).

Thornberry, Terence P. "Race, Socioeconomic Status and Sentencing in the Juvenile Justice System," *The Journal of Criminal Law and Criminology,* Vol. 64, No. 1, 1973.

Time, September 2, 1974.

"Toward A New Corrections Policy," *Crime and Justice,* Vol. 2 The Academy for Contemporary Problems, 1501 Neil Avenue, Columbus, Ohio 43201.

Tullock, Gordon. "Does Punishment Deter Crime?" *The Public Interest* No. 36, Summer 1974.

Uniform Crime Report 1972 (Washington, D.C.: U.S. Government Printing Office, 1973).

Vogt, Kraig, Director of Children's Services, Fort Mitchell Catholic Children's Home, Fort Mitchell, Kentucky, January 5, 1975 (interview).

Walker, Nigel, *Sentencing in a Rational Society* (New York: Basic Books, Inc., 1971).

Washington Post, February 17, 1975.

Wheeler, Gerald R., "America's New Street People: Implications for the Human Services," *Social Work*, Vol. 16, No. 3, July 1971.

Wheeler, Gerald R., "A New Policy of Juvenile Incarceration" (unpublished manuscript).

Wheeler, Gerald R., "A Study of Client Characteristics, Egalitarian Orientation and Institutional Factors Related to Response Pattern to Public and Voluntary Free Health Services," (unpublished dissertation) The University of Chicago, The School of Social Services Administration, March 1974.

Wheeler, Gerald R., "Children of the Court: A Profile of Poverty," *Crime and Delinquency*, Vol. 17, No. 2, April 1971.

Wheeler, Gerald R., "National Analysis of Institutional Length of Stay: The Myth of the Indeterminate Sentence," *Monograph*, Ohio Youth Commission, 1974.

Wheeler, Gerald R., and Harvey Inskeep III, "Youth in the Gauntlet," *Federal Probation*, Vol. 32, No. 4, December, 1968.

Wilkins, Leslie T., "Directions for Correction," *American Philosophical Society*, Vol. 118, No. 3, June 1974.

Williams, Paul N., "Boys Town: An Expose Without Bad Guys," *Columbia Journalism Review*, Vol. 13, No. 5, January/February 1975.

Wizner, Stephen, "The Child and State: Adversaries in the Juvenile Justice System," A symposium edited by Columbia Human Rights Law Review (Fairlawn, N.J., R. E. Burdick, Inc. 1973).

Wolfgang, Marvin, Robert M. Figlio, and Thorsten Sellin, *Delinquency in a Birth Cohort* (Chicago: University of Chicago Press, 1972).

Zimring, Frank, *Perspective on Deterrence* (Washington, D.C.: U.S. Government Printing Office, 1971).

INDEX

179